Welfare,
Justice,
and
Freedom

Welfare, Justice, and Freedom

Scott Gordon

Columbia University Press

New York   1980

Library of Congress Cataloging in Publication

Gordon, Howard Scott, 1924–
  Welfare, justice, and freedom.

  Includes bibliographical references and index.
  1. Political ethics. 2. Welfare economics.
3. Justice. I. Title.
JA79.G65   320′.01′1   80-14571
ISBN 0-231-04976-5

Columbia University Press
        New York   Guildford, Surrey

Contents

Preface

THIS BOOK BEGAN a long time ago, perhaps when I was an undergraduate at Dalhousie University in the early 1940s and was introduced to the subject of political philosophy in a seminar course conducted by R. A. Mackay. As a graduate student I did economics and during the early years of my teaching career I worked mainly in the fields of economic theory and economic policy. But my interest in political philosophy was not lessened thereby and my sabbatical leave year of 1963–64 was devoted entirely to reading in that field with the hope of doing some constructive work by joining economic theory and political philosophy together in some way. In 1970, in my summer course at Queen's University on the history of economic theory, I gave some lectures on the political philosophy writings of leading economists. This later developed into a course entitled "Welfare, Justice, and Freedom" which I have conducted in recent years at Indiana University. The lectures in that course have focused mainly upon the political philosophies of economists such as Frank Knight, Milton Friedman, Henry Simons, F. A. Hayek, J. M. Clark, J. A. Schumpeter, and James Buchanan, and also those of professional philosophers who have made extensive use of economics, such as John Rawls and Robert

Nozick. I have usually prefaced the study of these authors with some discussion of the concepts of welfare, justice, and freedom designed to clarify the basic issues of political philosophy and to indicate to students the nature of my own views, as a preliminary to a critical discussion of the assigned authors. This consideration of basic concepts grew into the extended essay which constitutes this book.

I am indebted to many students for critical and suggestive comments but I especially want to thank Richard Stout, Bruce Fletcher, and Michael Toman. For comments on this text and earlier drafts (or parts thereof), I also want to thank S. F. Kaliski, Dan Usher, Lloyd Orr, T. K. Rymes, Jack Wiseman, James Buchanan, Kenneth Boulding, George Stigler, Frank Milligan, and Nicholas Spulber. Linda Steinwachs did most of the typing with a degree of accuracy and speed that made the mechanical aspects of producing the book much less burdensome.

The editors of *Daedalus* have granted me permission to make use of my article on "Ideas of Economic Justice" which appeared in that journal's summer 1963 issue. The Economic Council of Canada has given me permission to make use of my paper on "The Demand and Supply of Government: What We Want, and What We Get" which was issued by the Council as Discussion Paper 79, February 1977.

H. S. Gordon
February 1980

Welfare, Justice, and Freedom

Politics One
and
Value
Judgments

The Nature of Politics

IN THE BOOK OF GENESIS, the story is told of how man became the accursed animal. Having disobeyed the governance of God, he was thenceforth condemned to govern himself, and to do so outside the gates of Eden where the economic law of scarcity applied, with its corollaries of choice and conflict. He carried with him into exile knowledge of good and evil, but it was not knowledge of *what* is good and *what* is evil, only a general realization that the two are distinguishable, the responsibility for differentiating specifics being his own. So he became the political animal, the economic animal, the moral animal, thrice cursed, while the serpent who had tempted him to disobedience was merely condemned to eat dust and go upon his belly.

The omnipresence of religious faith in human societies, and especially its intellectual elaboration in civilized ones, is a testament to man's yearning for the Edenic state. The Marxist theory that religion is simply a clever contrivance by which the sophisticated oligarchy keeps the ignorant masses quiet may have some truth in it, but it is a small part of the truth. Indeed, Marxism itself is only the most recent of the great organized religions to grow powerful through promise of Eden. But this focus of human thought is not confined to religion and theology. The history of secular political philosophy also provides ample testament to the great allure of the idyllic state, in which man is released from the burden of self-government; where politics is unknown.

One of the standard forms of this longing for Eden is the philosophy of political absolutism: the Edenic state is restored by subordination to authority, handing over all the tasks of government to a man-God, a sovereign, who alone has freedom of choice and bears all the responsibilities, as well as the powers, of moral judgment. Needless to say, there has never been any lack of candidates for the God-role; power over others does not obey the law of diminishing utility, and intellectual sophistry is easily employed to demonstrate that the sovereign accepts his great burdens as a personal sacrifice, for the good of his subjects. Dictatorship is the simplest form of government, and the most common. Political experience, past and present, makes one skeptical of claims that it is the route to Eden or its close substitute, but such skepticism can only be expressed in societies where men have the responsibility of self-government, so it is heard most loudly where it is least needed; the supply of political criticism is inoptimally distributed.

A different form of Eden is found in the speculations of those utopian social philosophers who construct the idyllic state by placing man in an imaginary world that is freed from the curse of scarcity. Where there is unlimited plenty there is no need for choice, and no problem of conflict among men. This Eden is not a well-governed state; it does not need a government at all. Having ceased to be an economic animal, man need not be a political animal either, or a moral one, so the three curses of Adam are lifted at one stroke. Political philosophies of this sort would be mere exercises in social science fiction, material for intellectual diversion or amusement, were it not for the widespread belief that scarcity is a man-made contrivance, engineered by the rich to keep the poor in subjection. According to this view, the economic problem is solely one of distribution. Numerous revolutionary upheavals have proved false the hypothesis of such an easily-attained Eden. Invariably, the storehouses do not turn out to be stuffed with plenty; the nocturnal elves fail to restock them while the people are in peaceful slumber; and the state does not wither away. But the faith remains strong, impervious both to history and arithmetic, testifying that man is also the romantic animal, given to dreaming the impossible dream.

Utopianists construct their image of Eden by assuming away the economic problem. A different line of thought that has been prominent in Western intellectual history is in some respects less ambitious: the curse of scarcity is retained but an approximation to the Edenic state is nonetheless considered to be available in "the best of all possible worlds," i.e. one that is governed exclusively by natural laws. Man has no need to govern himself as a social animal because that can be done for him by the action of natural forces. The philosophical foundations of this view were effectively laid in the seventeenth century when scientists were beginning to demonstrate that the order of the physical universe was spontaneous, obeying laws of a special sort which required no lawmaker and which, with total detachment and impartiality, enforced themselves. G. W. Leibnitz elaborated this into a general doctrine of natural harmony, which Alexander Pope celebrated in his *Essay on Man* and Voltaire ridiculed in *Candide*.

The idea of a natural harmonious order has won many disciples of various sorts, naive and sophisticated, over the past two centuries: William Godwin, Henry Carey, Herbert Spencer, William Graham Sumner, Ayn Rand, and Robert Nozick, to name only a few. As a vision of Edenic restoration it is more important than simple utopianism, however, because some of its disciples (and some of its critics) have attributed to it foundations that are more substantial than scholastic metaphysics or a simple faith in the beneficent orderliness of nature. These foundations are presumed to be provided by economic theory, which is interpreted as having demonstrated that a regime of competitive markets can, by itself, produce a just and efficient management of the problems of scarcity without the intervention of the state. That some social philosophers, including some economists, have made such claims cannot be denied, but it is a gross misreading of the history of economics to characterize the theory of competitive markets as a natural harmony doctrine which advocates a policy of laissez faire. None of the great figures whose work has created the science of economics can be validly represented as holding such a view. Even Adam Smith, whose name is regarded by some as synonymous with laissez faire (the Germans used to call the doctrine *Smithianismus*) was more a critic of the specific policies of the government of his time than of government as such; his *Wealth of Nations* does not suggest that a competitive economy can work entirely by itself, without a framework of man-made laws, nor does it, when read as a whole, indicate that the role of the state can, or ought to be, confined to the protection of life and property, national defense, and the maintenance of civil order. The work of economists, initiated by Adam Smith in the eighteenth century, has succeeded in establishing the important proposition that market processes in which self-interested individuals engage in free exchange can indeed create a spontaneous order which deals with the problem of scarcity; but just as important is the companion proposition, which has been equally well established, that market mechanisms do not perform with technical perfection even in the solution of this limited task, let alone in those that involve moral issues, which man unavoidably must face in his post-Edenic state.

The three Edenic philosophies which I have sketched so far—authoritarianism, utopianism, and natural harmonism—have all been prominent in the intellectual history of the West, and they remain alive and influential in the modern day. Many times destroyed by experience and analysis, they arise, like the Phoenix from its pyre, to win new disciples and, in the case of the first of them, to dominate human societies. In societies with well-established democratic traditions, such as ours, their appeal is effectively constrained by rational criticism, but the tawdriness, disorder, and frequent ineffectuality of democratic politics constantly energizes the search for a route to Eden in the hope that, despite the disappointments hitherto, a way might yet be found to the idyllic state.

The thesis of this essay is that the problems which man faces as a social being cannot be solved, or even ameliorated, by Edenic thinking. We have to accept the curses of Adam and devote our efforts to learning how to live more civilized lives in a world that is irredeemably outside the gates of any paradise. Most important, this involves acceptance of *politics*, despite its manifold deficiencies, as an essential feature of social life. To advance beyond the obvious, however, it is necessary to make this thesis more specific. What *is* politics, and what is the role it has to play in civilized society? The answer to these questions can be more clearly stated if we consider yet another essentially Edenic philosophy, much more subtle than the three outlined above, and much more appealing to the modern rational intellect than those simple and ingenuous romances of perfection.

This fourth approach rests upon a belief that all the curses of Adam, economic, political and moral, can be converted into scientific problems, and all human predicaments thereby provided with technical solutions. The adherents of this view do not hold that a perfect social order can emerge from the spontaneous operation of natural law, but they argue that, nonetheless, there *are* natural laws of human behavior, which can be discovered by scientists, and applied by experts to social problems in the same way that engineers apply the laws of physics to the management and modification of natural phenomena.

There are some extreme forms of this view which, while perhaps not relevant to the realities of modern democratic societies, are worth some brief notice in the interest of more clearly elucidating the form which is relevant. In the history of modern Western thought, one of the most striking of these extreme forms is the philosophy of Comtean "positivism." During that great period of intellectual ferment which accompanied the French Revolution, the École Polytechnique in Paris became the main locus of enthusiasm for the idea that the burden of being the political animal could be lifted from man's shoulders by science and technology. First Saint-Simon and then, more explicitly, his disciple Auguste Comte, essayed to describe a route of Edenic restoration based upon what was then, and still is, the most impressive achievement of the human intellect. Comte looked forward to the day when man had fully emerged from the dark ages of theology and metaphysics into the bright light of positive science, when he would adopt a "religion of humanity" whose priesthood would be composed of graduates from institutes like the École Polytechnique, trained in mathematics, science, and engineering, and suitably indoctrinated with a firm faith in the infallibility of positivism. Politics would cease to exist, sloughed off in the final moult along with man's other primitivisms.

This extreme positivism, or "scientism" as F. A. Hayek calls it, is seldom encountered today as an explicit proposal. The American "Technocracy" movement of the 1930s (which stemmed more from Thorstein Veblen than from Comte) was a brief example, due probably to the seemingly intractable problems of the Great Depression. There are Comtean elements in both fascism and communism, but the doctrines of subservience to a "führer" or the so-called "dictatorship of the proletariat" are really examples of the first Edenic theme—authoritarianism pure and simple—rather than authentic positivisms. One may perhaps also discern Comtean elements in other places, such as in some of the recent proposals for "economic planning" or in the argument of J. K. Galbraith,[1] that since modern democratic societies are already dominated by the "technostructure" of bureaucracy in both private enterprise and government, it is rational to achieve a more orderly synthesis by welding the now dispersed centers of managerial power into one organized structure.

The importance of Comtism as an Edenic romance would be as small as that of utopianism or natural harmonism, if we could locate it only, with difficulty, in idiosyncratic corners of modern thought. But if we extend our search beyond the extreme and explicit forms, it becomes evident that it is a very widespread and powerful feature of the modern intellectual temper. Shorn of extravagances such as the "religion of humanity," the general idea that all human and social problems can be scientifically analyzed and technically solved has immense appeal, which in recent years has been enlarged and deepened by the great progress of the social and behavioral sciences. It can be truly said that "we are all Comteans now," since we invariably look to experts for the solution of all human predicaments, personal or social.

The replacement of politics by science and technology would be possible if Eve's apple had endowed man with umambiguous knowledge of what is good and what is evil instead of the mere realization that there is a distinction. Science is not irrelevant to such questions, and ethical philosophy is not merely hot air. Man's moral sense and sensibilities can be made more knowledgeable and more sophisticated; there is no need for him to remain a primitive barbarian in his efforts to deal with moral problems. But moral problems do not have "solutions" in the same sense that empirical and logical problems do, and the task of making choices that involve moral issues or value judgments cannot be performed by a technical contrivance, or handed over to experts.

Some political philosophers have accepted the above

view, but have restricted it to the determination of ends only, not applicable to the problem of selecting the means that are chosen to achieve those ends. Isaiah Berlin, for example, has argued that political philosophy remains a flourishing subject solely because of the large differences which continue to exist in men's views of what constitutes the social good. If such differences were resolved, the only problems that would remain would be technical ones of devising efficient means, which "are capable of being settled by experts or machines, like arguments between engineers or doctors."[2] A similar view underlies Lionel Robbins's famous definition of economics as dealing with the processes by which productive resources may be efficiently employed to serve *given* ends.[3] If such a demarcation could be drawn between means and ends it would be possible to determine which social issues are appropriately attacked by technical expertise and which are not soluble in such a fashion and must therefore be included within the orbit of "politics" as I have been using that term. It is, however, far from clear that a clean demarcation of this sort is possible, since means and ends are not independent of one another. Even if it were possible, in principle, to make such a demarcation, in order to make use of it we would have to locate its position in the empirical reality. Nature herself offers no disclosure of where such a demarcation lies and, in fact, determining its location is itself one of the vital tasks of politics. Since science cannot demonstrate unambiguously what questions are technical and what ones are matters involving value judgments, the political process must determine the scope of its own operations. Political processes are not infallible in this regard of course, any more than they are in other matters, and the amateur politician may be strongly tempted to deal with difficult problems by assigning them to technical experts. This does not change the inherent nature of the problem, however, it only hands over a part of the responsibilities of politics to technicians. In the final chapter of this essay I will argue that one of the most serious deficiencies of modern politics consists in a tendency to shift the demarcation between the political and the technical continuously in favor of the enlargement of the latter, with the result that the power of experts grows inappropriately large.

The theory of politics that results from these considerations may appear paradoxical, since it seems to say that politics is a way of solving what is inherently insoluble. If moral problems are insoluble by any method, why reject the scientific method and embrace the political one? The difficulty is due to the meaning that is attached to the word "solve." If a scientific or logical problem is once solved, it need never be solved again; the solution can be recorded, like a recipe, and retrieved from the information bank whenever it is needed. Once we learn how to find the roots of a quadratic equation, or to determine the elements of a chemical compound, or perform a kidney transplant, we do not need to discover how to do it again, and the handling of specific cases becomes unproblematic. There are no solutions *of this sort* for moral questions and, therefore, no recipes for making choices *of this sort*.

The problem of making moral choices does not go away because we cannot solve it. Politics is the method of "solution" if by this term we do not mean anything permanent at all. Social problems may be "solved" today only to return tomorrow and the next day, without end, and each time we have to work out the "solution" anew, informed of course by previous experience, but not released from the burden of making value judgments. We would have a more correct view of the role of politics in social life if we did not use the term "solve" in connection with such matters at all, but described political activity as "coping" with social problems, under no illusion that we will not have to cope with the same ones again and again.

Solving can be done, and is best done, by experts, but coping is amateurs' work, so there is wisdom in the democratic view that politicians should be laymen and that political office should be open to all. The importance of this principle can perhaps be underlined by considering its application in another field where nontechnical decisions must be made, that of judicial proceedings. The apparatus of the judicial process is replete with the expertise of those who have special training in law, but the vital role of determining guilt or innocence is reserved for laymen. Why do we regard it as essential that this decision be in the hands of amateurs? According to the orthodox theory of judicial proceedings, it seems especially strange, since the formal role of the jury is not to make value judgments but to render a determination concerning matters of *fact*. If we really followed this theory in practice, juries would be composed of people who are experts in the scientific assessment of empirical evidence: statisticians, epistemologists, psychologists, chemists, or masters of whatever expertise germane to the particular case. That one instinctively recoils from any suggestion that juries be staffed on such principles does not merely reflect an unthinking conservative preference for what is traditional, but a recognition that the role of the jury in a judicial proceeding is not, in actual practice, confined to the assessment of evidence. We insist that an accused be judged by his peers because the jury is responsible for making a decision to act, not a mere factual determination. The whole matter would be clearer if, instead of the foreman reporting that he and his colleagues "find" the accused guilty or not guilty, he were to say something like "having heard the evidence and arguments, we have decided that the accused should suffer punishment (or should not)." The reason why juries are necessary is not because factual evidence is often ambiguous. Scientists deal with ambiguous evidence too and they have special skills for assessing it. Moreover, we employ juries in important cases even when the facts are indisputable, which would seem to be peculiar if we really hold to the theory that the responsibility of the jury is to make a factual determination.

If this theory of politics is persuasive, one is then led to consider the nature of the regime by which man attempts to cope with those social problems that do not have technical solutions. This regime consists of the institutional arrangements that are established to perform the task of government, but it also includes something more: the philosophical principles which control the establishment of institutional structures and direct their specific operations. In a good economy, supply responds to demand, and in a good polity, the supply of government responds to the demand for it. Needless to say, the demand for government is demand for *good* government. The philosophical anarchist views *all* government as bad; the Hobbesian views *any* government as good because it is better than anarchy. But most men have good sense enough to eschew such sweeping propositions, and their appraisal of a government depends upon the extent to which it effectively and efficiently supplies what they want. Different men want different things, of course, but if one is excessively concerned that this diversity may, theoretically, be complete, it becomes impossible to make "social choices" among "individual values"; and one falls into the catatonic immobility of Arrow's impossibility theorem,[4] or the scholastic extravagances of Paretian welfare economics. Men are individuals, but they do live in societies, and, being altricial animals, their wants are not primitive preferences but the products of enculturation (though not completely so). In any particular society there is a considerable degree of commonness of ends, so Arrow's theorem is of interest mainly to the academic theorist; for the practical work of politics, it is much less significant.

The large degree of commonness of preferences which one finds in any society is not confined to particular material wants which originate from biological necessities; it extends also to philosophical principles. In any society, and especially in a free one, there is variety in the values men hold; homogeneity is not complete, but it is large enough to enable one to base an appraisal of the "public sector" on an examination of the degree to which it serves commonly held values. The first task in such an appraisal is to elucidate these common values. They constitute the general demands that lie beneath the specific demands for governmental action. In the next three chapters I shall try to identify the values which are commonly, though not universally, held in modern democratic societies with highly developed industrial economies, and to analyze the complexities inherent in these values that defy technological solution and therefore require the "coping" role of politics.

The Search for a Methodology of Morals

If we wish to evaluate the operations of government, which is not the same thing as describing or explaining them, we have to employ criteria of evaluation that are essentially *moral* in nature. In the everyday discussion of politics the main criteria that are employed are the moral principles that are widely held contemporaneously in the particular society in question. If this were a totally satisfactory procedure, the task of discovering criteria of evaluation would be an empirical matter and could most effectively be pursued in a scientific fashion. It is not totally satisfactory, however, since it seems clear that there is no warrant for accepting commonly held moral principles as good simply because they are commonly held, regardless of what they happen to be. Even in the everyday discussion of politics there appears some sense of the need for, and possibility of, improving the criteria of evaluation themselves, so an empirical sociology of morals in insufficient.

The view that underlies this essay is that while the sociology of morals is insufficient to provide evaluational criteria, it is the necessary place to *begin*. Progress in morals (as, indeed, in anything) means progressing *from where we now are*, and it consists of making small incremental improvements rather than great leaps. This is not, however, the view that underlies the traditional approach to moral and political philosophy. Since the dawn of human history philosophers have attempted to devise a methodology of morals that can generate valid criteria of evaluation independently of the beliefs that ordinary men embrace. A large amount of intellectual energy has been spent in this effort, continuing right down to the present day in the philosophical disciplines and the social sciences.

The simplest and oldest of these traditional methodologies of morals is what might be called "revelationism." In the opening pages of the Book of Genesis it is told how man became the moral animal, but in the Book of Exodus a way of escape from this burden is described. Moses returned from Mount Sinai with a list of moral principles derived directly from God. The validity of these principles does not rest upon their intrinsic merits or their pragmatic usefulness, but solely upon their divine origin. They are commandments by an unquestionable authority, not debatable, and hence the agonizing burden of moral debate is seemingly lifted. "Seemingly" because the history of man as political animal discloses no cessation of moral debate following this revelation of God's will; it was merely shifted to focus upon *interpretation* of the rules, which served only to disguise the fact that the moral merits of the rules continued to be an open question. This methodology of morals remained for a long time the dominant style of moral discourse, and the search for "authoritative" rules has not yet passed away, but since the Renaissance it has become increasingly out of tune with the prevailing intellectual temper, and philosophers have turned to other methodologies.

One of these is "naturalism," the view that moral principles may be derived by examination of nature in the same way as the laws that govern the physical universe are discovered. David Hume, in the eighteenth century, put the quietus to such efforts by pointing out that there is a fundamental qualitative difference between matters of fact and matters of value, and the latter cannot therefore be derived from the former. If we were to adopt a sociology of values without qualification we would be committing the "naturalistic fallacy," since this would mean that evaluative criteria are totally derivable by examining phenomena of fact, the values which men do hold in a particular time and place.

Another of these methodologies of morals might be

called "rationalism." Instead of patterning the search for evaluative criteria upon empirical science, it takes mathematics and formal logic as its model. Moral criteria are presumed to be deducible a priori because they lie within the structure of logical thought itself. The modern version of this has attempted to obtain evaluative criteria by linguistic analysis, which is expected to disclose the intrinsic meaning of basic moral terms such as "good" and "bad," "justice," etc. We have learned a great deal from these efforts to clarify moral thinking, but it also seems clear that the expectation that an objective set of evaluational criteria can be derived in this way is doomed to disappointment.

A fourth approach of this type is "proceduralism." All methodologies of morals could be described as procedural since all contend that there is a procedure that is appropriate to the problem of discovering moral principles. Even the approach which I adopt in this book is based on the contention that this is the appropriate way of going about that task. But proceduralism as a specific methodology of morals is less general than that. It argues that one can specify a procedure that is inherently moral as such; it then follows that whatever emerges from such a procedure is moral *because* it is the result of a moral process, and for no other reason. Robert Nozick and James Buchanan[5] have recently tried to construct basic political philosophies employing such a methodology of morals. They argue, in different ways, that if we examine the process that would take place when rational self-interested men live under conditions of unrestrained individual freedom, we will find that certain developments would ineluctably ensue. These developments are proper, not because they themselves have moral merit, but because they result from a process which has. The main weaknesses of this approach are: (1) There is no warrant for claiming that any particular procedural process is the only one that is inherently moral. Working with very similar primary assumptions Nozick and Buchanan describe two quite different procedures, and these do not exhaust the possibilities. (2) Even if there were only one proper procedure, it is difficult to show that it generates unique conclusions, except in a tautologous fashion. (3) Common judgment does not accept as compelling the proposition that *whatever* emerges from a proper procedure is proper without any reference at all to its own characteristics. That is to say, hardly anyone is willing to abandon his right, so to speak, to judge the moral quality of the results of procedures as well as the procedures themselves. Indeed, it is more common, and more sensible in my view, to judge the merits of a procedure according to the results which it generates rather than the other way around.[6]

Proceduralism is unacceptable as a methodology of morals, but there is no doubt that it plays a large role in vernacular politics. Somewhat paradoxically, this is because it is not possible to establish value judgments on *any* firm and final base. We must cope day by day with the problems that arise in social life without certainty of what is best, but even "coping" would be well nigh impossible if we undertook to handle each problem de novo without making any use of precedent or established procedures. The political system is itself an established procedure, as is the judicial system and many other social activities. We cope with many problems, crime for example, by processing individual cases through an established procedure and acting on the results it generates. Social reform consists in large part of attempting to improve the quality of procedures, but it is quite clear that we evaluate that quality, over the longer run, in terms of the results produced. In the activity of day to day it is necessary that the great bulk of the population should accept the results of established procedures, obeying laws, for example, simply because they are laws; but in a longer view it is important to ask whether the results of the system are morally or socially acceptable. If the system works badly in some important respect, generating results that offend moral sense, there will be dissatisfaction with the structure of established procedures and demands for their revision. Under certain circumstances it may even be legitimate to engage in civil disobedience if that is necessary in order to call attention to the fact that established procedures are producing unacceptable results.

There are dangers in this view since it seems to open the door for anyone who is offended by the results of established procedures to apply, without constraint, as much power as he can command: taking hostages, bombing buildings, assassinating political leaders, etc. Even societies where power is widely shared and whose institutions are open to reform suffer from the activities of a small number of people whose sense of outrage has a low threshold and who do not regard it as necessary to consider the moral judgments and personal welfare of others. The view that only results count in moral evaluation also opens the door to procedural reforms which may be immoral in themselves. The practice of reverse discrimination in, say, selecting applicants for professional schools, is justified by its proponents as a means to produce desirable results. One cannot argue, on principle, that bad means *cannot* produce good results, but means and ends are both part of social activity and do not inhabit watertight moral compartments. Proper reform requires moral improvement of both the results and the procedures employed to achieve them. It is better to produce good results by good procedures than by bad ones. So, while there are severe deficiencies in the procedural methodology of morals. and in any architectonic political philosophy based on such a methodology, there is a great deal that can be said in favor of the view that procedures can be judged, partly, in terms of their inherent moral qualities.

Another approach to the methodology of morals is what K. R. Popper has called "moral futurism." This is closely related, on the one hand, to utopianism as a political philosophy and, on the other, to the doctrine that there are positive laws of history that determine the course of social development. If one believes that an ideal society can be constructed whose merits are infinitely superior to any existent one, then it seems clear that what is good and bad can be determined by reference to whether it contributes to or detracts from the achievement of this ideal. A contemporary action such as, say, terrorism, may seem to be evil according to the criteria generated by other moral methodologies, but it must be considered good if it contributes to the construction of the ideal society. The key term in this argument is the conception of the ideal society as *infinitely* superior to existing society. No magnitude can be larger than infinity, so no amount of present misery or palpable injustice can be regarded as more than dust in the balance when weighed against utopia. By such reasoning, the anarchists of the last century justified their actions as constituting "moral violence." Similar reasoning was employed by Catholic theologians during the Inquisition to justify torture in the name of the Christian doctrine of love: what weight has a few hours of agony if a soul can thereby be saved form the infinite torments of Hell and sent instead to the infinite bliss of Heaven?

Karl Marx did not believe in sketching the blueprint of utopia, but he did argue that there are laws of historical development, culminating in communism. Some of his followers have construed this to mean that the proper criterion of moral judgment is whether the action in question is in accordance with the inevitable course of history. Actions that run against this course are deplorable simply because they are fruitless; those who engage in them deserve moral condemnation because they embrace illusion instead of truth. By contrast, actions that are in accordance with historical law, even those that appear to be reprehensible by other criteria, are morally good because they are in tune with the inevitable. Inevitability plays the same moral role in this theory as the infinite value of the ideal plays in utopian theory.

Moral futurism obviously appeals to those who believe that social problems are only soluble by comprehensive social transformation. As a way of coping with the immediate problems of existent societies, its defects are gross. Historically, it has served to justify evil conduct rather than to define a set of moral principles which men can use to make social life more humane and more civilized. Its power as a moral theory is, however, very great. Doing violence to others is one of man's greatest pleasures but, now that he is half-civilized, he finds it necessary to justify the violence he commits. What can do so more effectively than the belief that his actions are sanctioned by a higher moral law? The theme of moral violence is the basis of modern political terrorism and war, but its scope is wider than this. It is, indeed, the most common scenario of the motion picture and the television screen: first one establishes the fact that someone has committed acts that are totally reprehensible; then it is possible to commit any degree of violence against *him* in the name of morality: the audience can give themselves up to the unrestrained enjoyment of *this* violence since it has been morally purified by justification.

Finally, we have to consider a sixth methodology of morals which shares with moral futurism the conception that actions must be judged in terms of their effects or consequences, rather than their origins or their intrinsic merits: "utilitarianism." This requires more extended discussion since it is by far the leading applied social philosophy of our age and, although it has serious defects, it also has some great merits which any alternative should seek to preserve.

Utilitarianism

The basic idea that underlies utilitarianism—that the criterion by which an action, a rule or practice, or an institutional arrangement, should be judged is whether it contributes to human happiness—is an old one, going back, like almost everything in Western social thought, to that great intellectual efflorescence that took place in Greece some two dozen centuries ago. The development of utilitarianism as an explicit social philosophy, and the use of it as a methodological foundation for social science, is much more recent, dating back not much further than the eighteenth century. In this brief discussion of utilitarianism, I want to focus upon the most important aspects of it which were developed by the English writers of this period: Jeremy Bentham, James Mill, John Stuart Mill, and Henry Sidgwick.

In his last will and testament Bentham described himself as "the author of the greatest happiness principle." In
this he was being neither modest nor accurate, but there is
no doubt that his development and promotion of the "principle" influenced modern Western social thought to an extent
that surpasses the efforts of any other single person.
Bentham really advanced *two* principles, not one: (1) the
positive psychological principle that man *is* by nature a
being who seeks (only) to increase his happiness; and (2) the
ethical principle that happiness is the (only) worthy human
objective—that which man, as a moral being, *ought* to seek.
The psychological principle became the foundation of "political economy," the first of the systematic empirical social
sciences; and the ethical principle become the foundation of
modern liberal democratic social and political philosophy.
In this discussion of utilitarianism I will focus upon those
features of it that led in these directions.

As a student at Oxford University, Bentham's main interest was in jurisprudence. Anyone with a taste for the psychological explanation of ideas could make a strong case
that Bentham's utilitarianism was a lifelong rebellion
against one of his teachers at Oxford, William Blackstone,
whose lectures, published as *Commentaries on the Laws of England* (1765-69), formed the first comprehensive synthesis of
English jurisprudence. The history of legal thought in England and countries whose legal systems are derived from
England (including the United States) was, during the nineteenth century, a struggle between Blackstone and Bentham,
with Blackstone constantly winning the allegiance of the
lawyers, but Bentham dominating thought in the other social disciplines and in practical politics. In the twentieth
century even the lawyers began to swing to Bentham's side,

a movement which has notably accelerated in the United States during the last twenty years with the growing interest of legal scholars in the findings of economists and sociologists and, most significantly, in the scientific methodology of modern analytical economics.

Blackstone held that the essential law of England was embodied in the decisions of judges and juries more than in the statutes passed by Parliament. He was not merely arguing that the English system of case law regards judgments on old cases as precedents that are germane to new ones; he viewed the accumulation of case judgments as embodying a steadily refined moral wisdom which was superior to any explicit ethical philosophy or any rational assessment. The moral merit of the law lies in its tradition. Good law is that which is continuous with customary practice. Reason is a fragile instrument whose serviceability in dealing with the complex problems of social life is severely limited, but man can draw upon something that is much more reliable: the mysterious wisdom of tradition.

For Bentham this was sheer mysticism. Customary practice might be morally defensible, but not because it was customary. The law is a human artifact which man makes, and changes, to serve his purposes. Whether the law is good or not has nothing to do with its history, but only with its consequences or effects, which must be rationally and empirically assessed according to the criterion of contributing to "the greatest happiness of the greatest number" of the members of society. Bentham applied this principle, not only to the law, but to all the institutions of society, including the state itself. All are mere artifacts, having no different status than a hammer or a pair of pliers, being good or bad according to how well they serve as instruments of happiness. Needless to say, it was difficult for most of the established social institutions of Bentham's time to pass such a test; their failure to do so made the nineteenth century into the Age of Reform, which continues to the present day.

It would be an erroneous reading of history, however, to attribute the political and social progress of the modern era solely to the intuitive appeal of the "greatest happiness principle" and the inability of established institutions to demonstrate utilitarian credentials. The most significant feature of the Age of Reform is not that it embraced human happiness as the criterion of morality, but that this was construed to be most fully and securely promoted by a polity that is democratic and liberal. Utilitarianism as a social philosophy is not *inherently* democratic or liberal. One can easily argue that a dictatorship is the most efficient way of producing the greatest happiness of the greatest number, and any despot can claim that "true" happiness consists not in the people being free to promote their happiness as they themselves perceive it, but in having what *he*, in his superior judgment, considers to be in their best interest. Thomas Hobbes can even be regarded as a utilitarian in the sense that he argued that since men are miserable in a state of anarchy, the establishment of a sovereign with unrestricted power to compel obedience and enforce order is a necessary condition for the promotion of the greatest happiness of the greatest number. Utilitarianism could have become a philosophy of repression, yet another of those political monstrosities which do not hesitate to offer unlimited human sacrifices upon the altar of the abstract greatest good. The Christian doctrine of indiscriminate love underwent such a transformation; the doctrine of national self-determination, once the great hope of people who were subject to foreign oppression, proved to be no bulwark against the emergence of equally or even more inhumane domestic tyrannies; Marxism, which promised to free man from the exploitative wage slavery of the capitalist market place, turned him instead into a slave of dictatorial politics. If the doctrines of love and freedom could suffer such radical metamorphoses, there is no reason to assume that the same could not have happened to the doctrine that human happiness is the fundamental moral good.

Bentham's philosophy, however, became in fact a powerful intellectual support of democratic liberalism. The sources of this development were many, the most important being the economic changes that were taking place under the impact of the industrial revolution. It would be a gross exaggeration of the independent role of ideas in human history to attribute the growth of democratic liberalism solely to Bentham and his disciples, but this book is about social philosophy, not history, so I will concentrate upon the intellectual developments in utilitarian philosophy that oriented it to the support of democracy and freedom in the Age of Reform.

James Mill, friend and disciple of Bentham, perceived clearly the crucial weakness of the argument that the greatest happiness of the greatest number could be efficiently promoted by dictatorial power. Moreover, he argued against it on the basis of that utilitarian principle that became the foundation of analytical social science. In his *Essay on Government* (1820) Mill applied Bentham's psychological principle that man is by nature a self-interested being to the problem of determining the best form of government. For practical reasons, all government involves the exercise of power by the few over the many. Since those who govern, like all other men, seek to serve their own interests, it is an illusion to believe that good government will result from placing power in the hands of benevolent men. No men are benevolent, and none are satiable in their desire to exercise power over others. Accordingly, the problem of government is one of constitutional design: one must construct a political order that assures that the only way in which those who hold power can serve their own interests is to act in ways that promote the greatest happiness of the greatest number. Reasoning this way, James Mill advocated that power should lie in the hands of representatives elected on the basis of a broad franchise (or broad at least by the standards of the time, well before even the Reform Bill of 1832). In this way, with frequent elections, those who hold power will be aware that they can only continue to hold it if they serve the wants of the electorate, and so their own interest becomes identical with the general interest.

James Mill was, clearly, somewhat overly optimistic about the virtues of representative democracy. It is difficult to discard altogether the view that good government requires public-spirited men as much as it requires ones who walk in constant fear of losing the next election. Nevertheless, his basic argument, if it is regarded as advancing the view that representative democracy, though not perfect, is a better constitutional order than any other, is a sound one. Moreover, his view that one must assume that men are self-interested, while incomplete, is a workable assumption for the scientific analysis of social phenomena. Economics is based upon it and, though it has often been attacked and decried, no alternative view has demonstrated an equal capacity to serve as foundation for the systematic study of man as a social animal. Curiously, the study of political processes, the subject with which James Mill's *Essay* was concerned, did not follow his lead in this respect. Only since the early 1960s has the utilitarian psychological principle been applied, with analytical rigor, to the examination of political processes and to Mill's central concern, the constitutional design of institutions through which power is exercised.

Democratic liberalism may be contrasted with dictatorial politics in terms of their structures of political organization but even more fundamental is the difference in the degree of intellectual freedom which they allow. In a dictatorial regime, the most offensive of all evils is *heresy*. The minions of power are sensitized to recognize its faintest odors and they labor conscientiously to cleanse the sources from which it emanates. And why not? Why should error be tolerated and its misguided or evil authors permitted to corrupt the minds of others? John Stuart Mill, James Mill's son, undertook to answer these questions in his essay *On Liberty* (1859).

John Mill argued, to begin with, that the most pernicious error was the belief that truth is already known, especially with respect to moral and social questions. Progress in these matters is possible and needful, and it can only be achieved by the advocacy of new ideas and the critical appraisal of established beliefs. Truth, though it can never be pure, can be progressively refined if it is made malleable by the heat of controversy and hammered on the anvil of rational debate. The empirical soundness of this view is hardly contestable when applied to scientific matters, but with respect to moral issues it can only appeal to one who is blessed by the possession of philosophic doubt. For those who are certain that what is good and what is bad are already known it can carry little weight. For them, however, John Mill advanced another argument. Moral truths, like scientific ones, will harden into dogmas unless they are subject to the heat and hammer of debate. Even those who are certain of the truth must want it to be an animating force in men's lives rather than a lifeless canonical doctrine which is embraced unthinkingly and repeated mechanically like a paternoster. To know the truth then, is insufficient; criticism, even to the point of heresy, serves to complement it; it vitalizes truth, keeping it abloom with the freshness and energy of youth.

One should note that John Mill did not defend freedom of thought and expression on the ground that man has a "natural right" to them or because they are intrinsically good in themselves. The argument is utilitarian; these freedoms are *useful:* they are like a knife and fork, instrumental in the service of worthy human purposes; not ends in themselves but means in the service of something other than themselves. Mill's argument is a strong one and it was a major contribution to the development of democratic liberalism as a social and moral philosophy. But I do not think that it really penetrates to the center of that philosophy since, in my understanding at least, democratic liberalism holds that man *does* have a natural right to freedom, and that freedom is intrinsically good; the burden of demonstration does not lie upon the advocates of freedom but upon those who question it. Later in this book, I shall adopt the view that freedom is a primary social good, which may indeed be instrumental to the attainment of other goods but must also be treated as an end in itself. I will come to the conclusion that intellectual freedom, and freedom to participate in political processes, enjoy an unambiguous status, but I arrive at this by a different route from that taken by John Mill.

Before we leave John Mill's defense of liberty we should

note one of its features more explicitly than we have so far done. The argument is based upon a belief in the constructive, progressive, and vitalizing power of *competition*. It brings into social and political philosophy the same view that Adam Smith had adopted in laying the foundations of economic analysis. Some opponents of democratic liberalism, perceiving this, regard the social philosophy of democratic liberalism as merely a reflection of the developing market economy of the nineteenth century. I would accept that contention in large part, except for the "merely." To some minds, competition is the antithesis of cooperation and must be stamped out of social processes and removed from man's psyche if a humane civilization is ever to be achieved. This is, in my view, erroneous on both scientific and philosophical grounds. Adam Smith argued that economic competition and cooperation are not inherently antithetical; given appropriate conditions they are complementary. James Mill's *Essay on Government* and John Mill's *On Liberty* were efforts to show that the same is true of political and intellectual competition. Whatever the defects of their arguments, that feature of them is valid, and of crucial importance to social philosophy.

The last of the utilitarian philosophers I want to consider in this brief discussion is Henry Sidgwick, late-nineteenth-century Cambridge classicist, philosopher, and economist, whose *Methods of Ethics* (1874) has exerted a continuing influence on moral thought. Sidgwick's utilitarianism was very different from James Mill's. Mill adopted the view that man is unalterably self-interested and took the main problem of politics to be that of constructing a constitutional order that would operate for the common good in a society of self-interested individuals. Sidgwick regarded man as capable of adopting unselfish modes of behavior and set himself the problem of defining the moral principles which, if employed as guides of individual conduct, would produce the greatest measure of general happiness in society. Mill was a theorist of political structure; Sidgwick was an ethical philosopher. The aspects of Sidgwick's ethical theory most germane to this discussion have to do with the economic issue of the proper distribution of wealth and income and the political issue of the distribution of power.

Bentham's ethical principle that happiness is the only good, when construed to mean that the sole criterion of social practices and policies is the maximization of aggregate happiness, does not permit one to make any independent value judgment concerning the distribution of that aggregate. If, in a society of two persons, one is ecstatically happy while the other is minimally so, it cannot be asserted that it would be a better arrangement if there were a greater degree of equality in the distribution of happiness, unless such a redistribution would raise the aggregate. It is not correct to say, as some interpreters of utilitarianism have, that utilitarianism is indifferent to or disregards the distribution of happiness (or income or power). What is implicit in the utilitarian philosophy is that distribution, as such, does not have any ethical merit; that specific distribution is best, whatever it may be, which maximizes the achievable aggregate. Sidgwick was convinced that human happiness is good, and the more of it the better, but he was unwilling to accept the distributional implication of Bentham's ethical principle. If, in our hypothetical society of two persons, each were to disregard the condition of the other, they would be practicing "egoistic hedonism," which Sidgwick regarded as morally unacceptable. Instead he argued for "universalistic hedonism," the adoption by each person of the view that the other person's happiness is *as* important *to him* as his own. This does not require the abandonment of the greatest happiness as an ethical principle; it means that in considering what will maximize it one must not discount the happiness of others solely because they are *others*. If Alfred will be made more happy by a piece of pie than Bertha he should have it; Bertha herself is ethically obligated to give it to him without recourse to any considerations other than the capacity of the pie to generate happiness. If Bertha's ability to turn pie into happiness is greater than Alfred's, even though she has already eaten two pieces and Alfred none, she is ethically obligated to consume the next piece herself. Neither self-sacrifice nor selfishness are permissible in Sidgwick's moral world.

The difficulties of Sidgwick's prescription are severe. In order to determine which of them should have the pie, it is not sufficient that Bertha should disregard characteristics that are palpably irrelevant, such as Alfred's sex or the color of his skin, she must be able to compare his "utility function" with her own. This is difficult to do within a small social organization such as a family whose members are well known to one another; the difficulties increase enormously as one widens the domain to embrace other members of society, including, as Sidgwick did, those of future generations. The doctrine that one must not discount others because of their social distance from ourselves or because of their distance from us in time is an unworkable rule of conduct. F. Y. Edgeworth, who was a great admirer of Sidgwick's *Methods of Ethics*, thought that it was theoretically possible to make quantitative measurements of happiness and he was confident that, some day, the problems of social life would be solved by experts in "hedonometry," but it is doubtful that even he expected that experts would be able to chart the utility functions of those not yet born. At any rate, analytical social science did not attempt to construct a method of utility measurement; the development of modern economics was based instead on the view that interpersonal comparisons of utility, or happiness, are not scientifically legitimate and that any social philosophy that requires such comparisons is untenable.

Sidgwick's contribution to the political philosophy of democratic liberalism would have been negligible if he had been content to advance his doctrine as a superior ethical intuition, regarding the practical problems of implementing it to be none of his concern. His most important contribution to democratic liberalism resulted from his effort to deal with the deficiencies of his own doctrine of universalistic hedonism, the crucial issue being that of determining the proper distribution of economic goods and political power.

An ethical person may be morally obligated not to *discount* the happiness of others but, Sidgwick recognized, this tells one nothing about the proper distribution since that is dependent upon an empirical matter, the utility functions of different persons. If one rejects Edgeworth's view that it is possible to construct a scientific "hedonometry" which will provide this empirical information, one must, instead, make some *assumption* about utility functions. If no specific assumption is more tenable than any others, then utilitarian social philosophy cannot provide arguable guides for social policy on the basis of the greatest happiness principle. Concerning the distribution of economic goods, for example, it is logically demonstrable that different assumptions concerning utility functions lead to quite different distributional conclusions. If Albert's utility function and Bertha's are identical, and both are characterized by diminishing marginal utility, then it follows that the aggregate happiness will be maximized by an equal distribution of the available pie. If the utility functions are identical, but characterized by constant marginal utility, it does not matter how the pie is distributed; all distributions generate the same aggregate. If Albert and Bertha equally enjoy the first bit of pie but Alfred's marginal utility is constant while Bertha's diminishes, then maximizing aggregate utility requires that Albert get virtually all of the pie and Bertha virtually none. Other assumptions about utility functions lead to the conclusion that the proper distribution of pie depends critically on how big the pie is; for example, it is easy to construct a case, without making psychological untenable assumptions, in which if the pie is very small or very large it should be shared very unequally, but if it is of an intermediate size, equality is indicated. The utilitarian ship of state would seem to be afloat upon an uncharted sea; no one knows how to set a course for the lovely land of maximum happiness since it can lie in any direction. But *some* course must be set nonetheless. Is it possible to do so by arguing that one of the possible assumptions about utility functions is more tenable than any other? Sidgwick did not attack this problem in the explicit analytical terms I have employed in this paragraph but he was able to make a powerful argument on behalf of equality of distribution. What is most important to the philosophy of democratic liberalism, however, is not his egalitarian conclusion, but the argument itself.

If we cannot make empirical utility comparisons in order to determine the proper course for social policy, then any course we do set is very likely to be in error. But there is no reason to think that all are subject to the same degree of error. If it is determinable that one assumption about utility functions is exposed to less error than any other, it is plausible to contend that this is the one that should be adopted. This is the prudential "minimax" rule of modern decision theory: adopt the policy that minimizes the maximum error exposure. Sidgwick's argument was intuitive, but it was in substance the same as that of the explicit logic of decision making which has since been developed. The argument is undoubtedly well known to some readers of this essay but it is worth a bit of explication in order to highlight the import of Sidgwick's contention.

Suppose that one is a participant in a game of chance which consists of making blind draws from a box in which someone has placed black and white balls. If information is given concerning the proportion of black to white balls in the box, the chance of losing is minimized by making one's bet in accordance with that information. If the proportion in the box is known to be two-to-one in favor of black then one should expect that, in a series of draws, black will be drawn twice as often as white, and bet accordingly. But suppose that one is given no information at all concerning the proportions; what *assumption* minimizes the maximum risk of loss? The rational gambler should proceed on the assumption that the chances of a black being drawn is the same as a white. This is the same assumption it would be rational to adopt if one *knew* that white and black were in equal proportion. (Utopianists are, by contrast, not rational gamblers. They always bet their "favorite" color regardless of the odds against it. They prefer any small chance of being right over any large chance of being wrong. Or, they proceed with confidence that they know what color will be drawn regardless of the empirical facts, or the lack of them. Utopianists, in effect, are either imprudent in the face of known facts, or they regard facts as irrelevant.)

The important point about this is that rational analysis prescribes that when one knows nothing about a distribution, the minimum exposure to error is achieved by acting on the assumption of equal probability. Sidgwick argued this way concerning utility functions. If we know nothing about the utility functions of Alfred and Bertha, the proper distribution between them is the same as if we know them to be identical; the pie must be equally shared.[7] (Sidgwick did not note explicitly that it is also necessary to assume that the marginal utility diminishes.) In Sidgwick's view, this leads one to unambiguous conclusions in the domain of politics. All members of society must be presumed to be equally capable of exercising political power. There is, therefore, no warrant for restricting the franchise or other opportunities for participation in political processes. Sidgwick did not contend that all persons *are* equally wise, equally competent, or public-spirited to an equal degree. It is not necessary to make such a questionable empirical assertion in defence of democratic liberalism; it is sufficient to recognize that empirical assessment of comparative political worth is impossible. Everyone must be *assumed* equal in the political domain because those merits are hidden from view, and will always remain so. The ship of state minimizes the chances of sailing into absurdity when all aboard have an equal opportunity to participate in the collective decision-making process.

In effect, Sidgwick's political theory is based upon the recognition of ignorance. This is difficult for the intellectual to accept but it is even more important to the defense of democratic liberalism today than in Sidgwick's time for, in the intervening century, the intellectual class has come to power, and there is little evidence that its modern members have rejected the Platonic or Comtean view that a good society is one in which power is concentrated in the hands of the proper elite. In the following chapters of this book I shall adopt Sidgwick's view that a rational and progressive political philosophy requires the recognition of ignorance as much as it requires sustained and sophisticated efforts to increase our knowledge about social phenomena and human values. What must be rejected is not the aspiration to learn more but the desire for *simplicity*. Philosophic doubt springs from the awareness of complexity; the recognition of ignorance does not mean that we know nothing, but that the more knowledge we acquire the more we reveal the complexity of the worlds of facts and values. My object in the following chapters will not be to offer yet another methodology of morals to replace utilitarianism and other simplicities, but to examine the basic concepts of Western social philosophy in their untidy heterogeneity.

There is another issue raised by Sidgwick's interpretation of utilitarianism which we must consider before leaving him. The observant reader will have noted that the preceding discussion of whether utility functions may be compared was carried out in terms of the economic problem of the distribution of income, but in indicating the implications of the minimax principle attention was shifted to the political problem of the distribution of power. Sidgwick was well aware that parallel arguments can be made on these two issues. If the minimax principle requires one to regard all members of society as equally worthy political entities, why does the same reasoning not compel one to conclude that the best distribution of income is a perfectly equal one? Sidgwick was emotionally drawn to egalitarianism in all respects, but he rejected equality of income on the ground that such a rule of distribution would seriously impair the productive efficiency and growth of the economy. Economic goods must be produced in order to be distributed, and if their production requires human activities that will not be undertaken unless rewarded, it follows that the best distribution may not be an equal one. The production system is interwoven with the distribution system in a complex way, since distributions act as production incentives. This is an exceedingly important issue and one in which we can make no headway without the assistance of economic analysis. This alone is sufficient to make economics a vital constituent of social philosophy. But it raises the more general problem of the conflict of goals, which is the fundamental reason why simplicity cannot serve as an acceptable criterion for a methodology of morals that can be employed as a guide to social action and reform.

So far, in this discussion of utilitarianism, I have been mainly concerned to argue the merits it acquired at the hands of Bentham's followers. These are so great, and they are so superior to those of any other social philosophy so far constructed, that one cannot easily abandon it. It has deficiencies, however, which are serious and cannot be repaired. The utilitarian code served us well during the first century or so of the Age of Reform, but it is now time, in my opinion, to take leave of it. The direction in which I believe we can fruitfully go is argued in the remainder of this essay. As an introduction to that discussion I go on now to a brief review of the deficiencies of utilitarianism which have led me to adopt an approach to social philosophy that is quite different from that of those who seek solutions in the further development of utilitarianism through Paretian welfare economics or the construction of a "social welfare function," or in the adoption of any of the nonutilitarian methodologies of morals outlined earlier in this chapter.

The most fundamental of the deficiencies of utilitarianism is that the concept of "happiness" cannot be supplied with meaning that is concrete enough to meet the practical needs of social policy. Bentham attempted to make it more concrete by designating "pleasure" and "pain" as the positive and negative constituents of happiness and by suggesting that these could be evaluated in terms of definite quantitative dimensions such as intensity, duration, number of persons involved, etc., and Edgeworth looked towards the development of a science of hedonometry as the way of making utilitarianism into a serviceable social philosophy. When neoclassical economists abandoned the idea of making quantitative measurements of pleasure and pain they did not discard the basic Benthamite view that happiness is the sole good, but in attempting to give it a serviceable degree of concreteness they construed it in a way that empties it altogether of meaningful ethical content. They in effect discarded Bentham's ethical principle and attempted to make his psychological principle serve in its place. Happiness, or "utility," as economists began to call it, is not definable or measurable in any "social" sense, but if we assume that Bentham's psychological principle is sound it follows that each individual determines his own utility for himself and his actions reveal the result of his assessment. We cannot make any ethical judgments concerning those actions because the only indicator of what is good is provided by the actions themselves. This fails to recognize that a serviceable social philosophy requires two types of statements: positive statements containing the verb *is* and ethical statements containing the verb *ought*. No social philosophy is serviceable if those are construed to be either totally disjunctive or identical. If disjunctive, they are irrelevant to one another; if identical, they are similarly irrelevant because no difference between them is discoverable. Bentham's psychological principle becomes a tautology in the hands of neoclassical economists, since "utility" has no independent definition of its own. One need not deny that the individual is the best judge of what serves his wants (assuming certain conditions concerning information available to him) but to say that he maximizes "utility" is merely to say that he maximizes "something," which is ineffable. The "something" may be labeled with any word or symbol we may choose but it is not capable of being described or analyzed. The independent and dependent variables of a utility function are not different things, but different names for the same thing.

Even if utility were definable nontautologically, indeed even if it could be measured quantitatively, the proposition that the proper object of social policy is to maximize the *aggregate* utility does not necessarily follow. Is a society with a large population and a low average utility better than one with a small population and a high average utility, if the aggregate utility of the former exceeds that of the latter? If the utilitarian confines attention to a society of given population he leaves an exceedingly important social problem, population policy, outside his domain, but he does not thereby preserve ability to deal with those problems that remain within it. In a society of given population, whatever maximizes aggregate utility also maximizes average utility, but there is no clear warrant for adopting these as the proper objects of social policy. The aggregate (and the average) utility is not the utility of anyone. The Paretian economist adopts this as the correct rule but he cannot defend its merits against other contentions. Why not maximize the modal or the median utility or the geometric rather than the arithmetic mean? Or, why not maximize the utility of the least advantaged members of society? The latter proposition has been advanced by that branch of utilitarian philosophy called "negative utilitarianism," by the philosopher of science Karl Popper, and by the ethical philosopher John Rawls. Such a rule has a strong widespread appeal, especially in societies where the general standard of living is high but pockets persist where it is very low, and it is not possible to show that this rule is inferior to the maximization of aggregate utility. Or, why not maximize the variance of utility, or its skewedness, or some other moment of its distribution? Plausible arguments can be made for these, and other, objectives. One can defend the rule of maximizing aggregate utility by adopting the view that "society" is an organic entity and contending that *its* utility is the proper objective of social policy. Economists who speak of "social welfare functions" may view this as the solution for the difficulties of utilitarianism, but it creates far more problems than it solves. In sum, utilitarianism begins with the view that happiness or utility is meaningful only for people as individuals, but it proceeds to adopt a rule—maximize aggregate utility—which does not apply to individuals and which even permits flirtation with the grossest forms of anti-individualistic social philosophy.

These defects of utilitarianism spring from its adoption of the view that all the various things that people value can be reduced, in principle, to one basic homogeneous value, called happiness or, in the theoretical models constructed by economists, utility. The mathematical formulation of these models tends to mask the fact that the basic value that is adopted is undefinable; "utility" degenerates into a vague "essence" or is defined tautologously as "that which everyone basically values."

The philosophical view that underlies this book does not attempt to replace the utilitarian approach by adopting some other single value as the fundamental human objective. Instead of searching for the simple homogeneous essence of all that is, we can more fruitfully proceed by recognizing the heterogeneous complexity of reality and the plurality of human values. Utilitarianism, as a psychological theory and as a moral methodology, is inadequate because it is monistic. It is a better social philosophy than any other type of monism, but we can, in my view, do better still by adopting a philosophy of *pluralism*. The remainder of this book is essentially an analytical essay on the social philosophy of pluralism. As an introduction to the following chapters, the next section will attempt to specify the main features of pluralism.

Pluralism

At the outset, I want to note that although I label the philosophy presented in this book as "pluralism" I am uneasy about doing so. This is not because the word is more misleading or more ambiguous than other philosophic terms, but simply because all labels used to represent philosophic systems tend to become slogans which suppress thought rather than verbal instruments which assist it. This is especially common when a denotative label degenerates into a political cliché or clarion call. A crowd of people shouting "Long Live Pluralism!" in unison would make me (almost) as uneasy as a crowd shouting "Long Live the Revolution!"

The tendency for denotative labels to lose their usefulness is especially severe when they are derived from a proper name. If, for example, a person describes himself as a "Marxist," this presumably means that he embraces the philosophy espoused by Karl Marx. We find, however, that many different positions are adopted by those who call themselves Marxists, some of them clearly contradictory. Some Marxists believe that there are "laws of history" governing the unfolding of events which cannot be broken by human action; others believe that the chief message of Marxism is that men should strive to alter historical processes; still others believe that the laws of history are unbreakable until they culminate in the emergence of communism, after which no laws of this sort are operative at all as constraints upon what man can do. Some Marxists believe that "exploitation" is the result of monopoly capitalism; others that Marxian economic theory shows that exploitation exists in a market economy characterized by perfect competition. Some Marxists believe that the doctrine of "the increasing misery of the working class" refers to a decline in the absolute material standard of living of the proletariat; others that it refers only to a *relative* decline of the proletariat compared to capitalists; others that it does not refer to material matters at all but to the psychological quality of life: that it is characterized by growing "alienation."

As a consequence, there is an enormous literature that aims at revealing what Marx himself really intended to say. Some of this is true intellectual scholarship, but other efforts are inspired by the desire to determine which Marxists are authentic and which are heretical. Some believe that the only way to separate true and false Marxists is to establish a single interpretive authority, such as the Politburo, or even more simply, the current chairman of the Communist party of the USSR. (Christianity went through the same process with the establishment of the doctrinal authority of the Curia Romana and the enunciation of the dogma of papal infallibility.) Marxists who reject the doctrinal supremacy of a central authority are of such diverse sorts that the philosophical garments they wear would seem to be custom-made to individual tastes, resembling one another only in the appliqué of common rhetorical ornamentation. Sir Ronald Meek, one of the leading British historians of ideas, became so disillusioned with what is signified by the term Marxist that he once remarked that he was no longer a Marxist, but had become a Meekist. Michael Harrington, the leading popular Marxist in the United States today, once noted, after describing what he understood by the term, that he himself may well be the only authentic Marxist in existence. One of Karl Marx's daughters remarked that her father was once moved by some of the doctrines being espoused in his name to say that he was not a Marxist.

This tendency for words to degenerate when used as labels is not confined to Marxism. The same problem is encountered with respect to such doctrines as Christianity, Benthamism, Keynesianism, liberalism, conservatism, socialism, and so on. Anyone who holds a pluralist philosophy should be especially aware of the stifling potentialities of the use of doctrinal labels, including the label "pluralism" itself. With that caveat, I will now go on to delineate the specifications which that label denotes in my own use of it. These specifications refer to four issues that are relevant to social philosophy, having to do with the pluralist concept of existence, ethics, politics, and economics.

Existential Pluralism

The idea that the world is, despite all appearances, a unity, the manifestation of an essential one-ness, is one of the most pervasive ideas in the history of human thought. The search for "the one that is in the many" has been the inspiration of many philosophers and religious thinkers in widely different cultures. In Western thought this conception of the nature of things was given a powerful impetus by Judaeo-Christian monotheism, which became the dominant religious tradition. In modern scientific thought it has been powerfully supported by reductionism, the view that the existential variety of phenomena results from combinations of less heterogeneous constituents, and these are in turn reduced, until at last we come to the homogeneous irreducible *one*. Thus the various forms of material things can be reduced to molecules, molecules reduced to atoms, and so on until we come to the "quark" for which physicists are now searching.

From the standpoint of what is relevant to social philosophy however, it does not matter if physicists find that all matter is composed of one basic entity. Existential pluralism rests upon the contention that, whether matter is homogeneous at bottom or not, mental phenomena are not reducible to physical or material elements; or, to put it differently, *ideas* are not reducible to *things*. Furthermore, *values* are not reducible to *facts*, even if the facts in question are phenomena of human behavior that are based on value judgments. Thus, for example, to say that "Smith killed Jones because he felt that Jones ought to have been killed" is not the same thing as to say that, indeed, "Jones ought to have been killed." The first statement is a statement concerning *facts;* the second is a statement concerning *values.*[8]

The existential world of a pea plant or even of a low-level animal such as a coral or a flatworm may be monistic, reducible totally to material elements, but as we go up the evolutionary tree, new kinds of elements emerge: organisms develop nervous systems controlled by brains. The large neocortex in the brain of *Homo sapiens* does not mean that we are no longer biological, chemical, and physical entities, but it does mean that man lives in a plural world in which, in addition to material things, consciousness and value judgments exist.

Ethical Pluralism
Religious thought, as I have indicated, is strongly monistic, but there is also a prominent pluralist strain in it since most religions aspire to control human conduct according to principles that establish what is good and what is bad. If goodness and badness are meaningful and distinct concepts, then the world, at the ethical level, is, at the least, dualistic rather than monistic. In Christian theology, this dualism is most strongly represented by Manichaeism, which regards the world, at the existential level, as characterized by a struggle between good and evil, or light and darkness.

Ethical pluralism is the doctrine that not only is there goodness and badness, but there are numerous *kinds* of goodness and badness, or numerous *criteria* by which goodness and badness may be judged. Man has the capacity to do more than classify phenomena under two ethical headings.

If the nature of things were such that all criteria of

goodness (and badness) were congruent with one another, it would not matter that there are numerous criteria since they would guide value judgments in a harmonious way. The basic problem of ethics arises from the fact that criteria of goodness may conflict with one another. The ethical pluralist accepts this and does not attempt to eliminate such conflicts by methods such as utopian reconstruction, reduction, or lexicographical ordering. The main tasks of pluralist ethics are to clarify ethical criteria, identify conflicts of values, and improve our ways of mediating them.

Political Pluralism

A solitary individual living all alone might have plural values, and conflicts among them might disturb his peace of mind, but no problem of how to resolve them would exist since he could establish for himself whatever procedure of choice he wished, and change that procedure at will. He could toss a coin, consult the stars, or make mathematical calculations, and shift from one method to another as suited his fancy.

For individuals living in a society, such arbitrary adoption of decision-making methods could still be employed for matters that concern only one individual, but not for ones that affect more than one. A person could use coin-tossing or astrology or mathematics to decide which shirt to put on in the morning, but decisions concerning what changes to make in the criminal law, or how much street cleaning should be done, or what foreign policy should be adopted, are different matters, since these decisions deal with collective concerns. Some method must be employed which is suitable for making what the current social science literature calls "public choices," and some procedure must be established which is suitable for *changing* the method by which such choices are made, i.e. making "constitutional choices."

The making of collective decisions in a world of conflicting values is the chief task of politics. Political pluralism is the doctrine that, since individuals differ in their values and their interests, collective decisions should be made by procedures which permit participation by all members of society. Direct voting on issues, by means of plebiscites, is a method for determining what a law or policy should be, but it does not provide for its day-to-day administration; continuing government is necessary, so voting must be for representatives who not only make decisions but oversee their implementation. The plural theory of politics holds that plural institutions of government are better than any monistic concentration of authority, so there should be many governments even within a nation: states, county councils, school boards, zoning boards, etc.

Contemporary public choice theory focuses mainly upon voting procedures and tends to neglect other important aspects of good collective decision-making. Even if plebiscitary democracy were feasible, or if representative democracy were effectively organized into plural institutions of government with an appropriate distribution of powers and responsibilities, reliance only upon voting is insufficient since those who are in the minority on a particular issue should have some influence on how it is resolved. The single individual should have opportunity to participate in the process in diverse ways: not only by voting, but also by trying to influence the views of others through discussion, and by participating in the activities of political parties, public interest groups, and various other associations that have impact upon the political process. Politics, then, is plural when there are many centers of political power, and when the individual members of society may participate in the process of collective decision-making through many different channels.

Economic Pluralism

The task of an economy is to employ productive resources in the production of goods and services. Every system of economic organization must determine what to produce, how to produce it, and how the resulting production is to be shared. In the pure-type "command" economy, all the relevant decisions are made by a centralized authority and transmitted as commands to the entities responsible for specific tasks. In the pure-type competitive market economy, individuals offer the productive resources they possess for sale to profit-seeking producing enterprises, and these enterprises offer their production for sale to individual consumers. The prices determined in these markets carry the information that is required to organize the process into a coherent whole.

No real economy is a pure type. The most centralized command economies, such as the USSR, make extensive use of markets as part of their systems of economic organization, and the most decentralized market economies, such as the United States or West Germany, make extensive use of the command mechanisms of government. Indeed, it is highly doubtful that either of the two pure types of economy could exist as stable states, and it is certain that neither of them would be an efficient method of using resources in the production of goods and services. All functioning economies are mixtures of command and market mechanisms.

This mixture is an essential ingredient of a plural economy but it is not a sufficient specification. The doctrine of economic pluralism holds that the proper object of economic organization is not merely to employ productive resources in the production of goods and services with technical efficiency, but to do so in a way that responds to the preferences of the individual members of society. People differ greatly in their preferences for goods and services and, moreover, every individual prefers a mixture of them rather than any single thing. An economy is pluralist to the degree that it is able to accommodate a variety of tastes, and the taste for variety.

These brief notes must serve, for the moment, as specifications of "pluralism." In the following chapters I will not engage in further exegesis of this label. My object is to clarify and analyze the complex of widely shared social values, which I will do by classifying them under the headings of "Welfare," "Justice," and "Freedom." Chapter 5 will then attempt to determine the ways in which these values may conflict with one another. The final chapter discusses a special problem which appears repeatedly in the preceding chapters: the organization of coercive power.

Two
Welfare

THE IDEA OF PROGRESS has received much attention from historians in their efforts to describe and explain the development of the modern intellectual temper. Like other ideas, it has long roots, but its forceful appearance on the intellectual scene is quite recent, accompanying the economic and political ascendancy of Western Europe, and societies derivative therefrom, over the past few centuries. For the ancient Hebrews, man could never aspire to greater heights than had already been experienced when he was under the direct governance of God in Eden. For many of the classical Greeks, history was an endless cycle at best, with no forward movement, and Plato thought that all change was decline. The overwhelming of Rome by the barbarian invasions established a conviction, lasting more than a millennium, that history is a record of regression, and the epidemics which swept across the human ecumene in the later Middle Ages sharpened the view that there was more woe than welfare in man's worldly experience. The rise of Islam did nothing to alter this view in Christian lands but it did not establish the concept of progress in Moslem society either, for the idea is a secular one, based upon the attachment of great value to the quality of mundane life. We owe the development of the idea to the economic growth and geographic expansion of Western Europe, now taken for granted as the dominant scenario of human development, but which came late, and rather inexplicably, upon the historical scene.

When the idea of progress began to take hold of the European imagination there was a great deal of discussion of what might serve as its indicator, since the concept itself is quite vague. There was a striking debate in the eighteenth century concerning the relative populousness of different times and places, since many believed that more progressive societies would contain more people. David Hume wrote a number of essays to show that there was progress, in one of which he argued his case by attempting to prove that the contemporary world was more populous than the ancient one.[1] He had no data, and his celebrated essay is more interesting as an example of how a clever mind can tackle an empirical problem without empirical facts than as a demonstration of progress. But the attempt to construe progress from population growth had a brief run, destroyed utterly by Malthus' *Essay on Population* (1798), which placed a different construction on the matter.

The modern observer of the social scene has command of much more empirical data than was available to Hume, but efforts to determine whether progress (or regress) has taken place is not greatly assisted thereby. I do not intend, in this discussion, to attempt any quantitative measurements, nor to lay down theoretical principles by means of which an index of progress can be constructed. The idea of progress is a highly synthetic one, embracing a heterogeneous mixture of elements which resist capture by any single indicator. The important task is to clarify what is in our minds when we make statements such as "there was a great deal of social progress in the 1960s" or "the Supreme Court decision in *Brown* v. *Topeka* was a progressive act" or "the Environmental Protection Agency is a progressive institution." In order to cut through the vagueness of such statements, we must unpack the omnibus term "progress" and examine the more concrete elements that are its constituents. In this chapter I will discuss those elements that can be classified under the heading "welfare." One should note at the outset, however, that it is extremely difficult to separate welfare considerations from those of justice, as the modern literature of "welfare economics" shows so clearly. Nevertheless, it is imperative to distinguish between them in order to examine either effectively. In what follows, I shall not be able to preserve a strict demarcation between welfare and justice, so the discussion in this chapter should be regarded as dealing with matters that *mainly* come under the heading of "welfare."

Welfare and Preferences

Modern economics does not restrict itself to the task of describing and explaining the empirical behavior of economic phenomena; and an essential part of its theoretical core is "normative," consisting of an attempt to evaluate that behavior and to locate opportunities for improvement. The concept of welfare plays a central role in normative economics and does so explicitly since the seminal work of A. C. Pigou, which laid down the analytical foundations of the subject a half-century ago.[2] Economists have been acutely aware of the difficulties involved in the concept of welfare and the tendency of this subject to become infused with moral philosophy. In an effort to limit this infusion and provide a basis upon which the analysis may proceed without being drawn into the quagmire of philosophical disputation, the mainstream of economic theory has constructed its normative model on a conception of welfare that is defined in terms of empirical preferences rather than moral precepts. The welfare of an individual person is considered to be increased whenever he is enabled to move from one state of affairs to another which, in his own private judgment, he prefers. The welfare of any social group is considered to increase whenever at least one member of that group is enabled to move to a preferred state without this entailing that any other member must move to a dispreferred state. The social welfare is maximized when all such opportunities to satisfy the preferences of some persons without negative effects on any other are realized. This is the principle of "Pareto optimality," which plays a large role in modern economics. By adopting this principle as the concept of welfare, the value judgments that economists must make are reduced to a minimum and, moreover, they harmonize with the methodology of individualistic utilitarianism which is employed in the analysis of empirical economic behavior, so there is no incongruity between the explanatory and the prescriptive branches of the subject.

Defining welfare in terms of individual empirical preferences has proved to be a powerful instrument of analysis and it is not my intention to denigrate it without offering a superior approach. However, it is subject to severe difficulties, which are the roots of some of the sharp controversies that have punctuated the modern discussion of social policies. The complexity of the concept of welfare is apparent when one considers the difficulties that attend the doctrine of Pareto optimality.

Defining welfare in terms of empirical preferences eschews any consideration of the independent moral merits of
such preferences and any consideration of the processes by
which they are generated. If human life were a simple struggle for biological existence, preferences would originate in
and be justified by the primal requirements of organic survival and species reproduction. But, with few exceptions,
man is far removed from such a state of existence. Most of
his wants are highly factitious. Even those based on biological necessities have developed a degree of sophisticated elaboration which, in almost all societies, dominates over primal
needs. The demand for food is not a simple matter of supply-
ing the organism with its metabolic requirements; we do not
eat, we "dine." The demand for clothing is not simply a
desire to assist the homeostatic mechanism in maintaining
temperature control; we do not wear clothes, we "dress."
The sex act is not only, or even mainly, a method for bringing sperm into contact with ovum; we "make love." Even
societies that are, by American standards, desperately poor,
devote most of their productive energies to satisfying preferences whose connection with biological necessities is much
attenuated. Since we cannot, therefore, attribute man's preferences to biological necessities, or justify them on grounds
of species survival, consideration of their origin and meritoriousness is necessary to any judgments of human welfare.

A long-standing debate in the literature of social philosophy focuses on the meritoriousness of empirical preferences
by drawing a distinction between man's "material" welfare
and his "cultural" or "spiritual" welfare. Insofar as the last
of these terms refers to other-worldly concerns it raises questions which I have no desire to pursue, the problems of *orbis
mundi* being sufficiently difficult. But the question of
whether cultural welfare may be differentiated from mate-

rial welfare, and whether they are congruent or conflictual, is an important issue even for an atheist. This differentation is not easy since, as I have already argued, there are few human wants that do not have a large cultural superstructure, but the distinction between material and cultural welfare is nonetheless an intelligible one (if not rigidly drawn) since it is clear that some wants are more material than others. The important issue however is whether these different components of welfare are in a condition of congruence or conflict. If they are congruent (either being independent of one another or complementary to one another) no serious problems arise and there is little point in trying to draw a distinction between them. If they are in conflict, however, we face great difficulties in the analysis of welfare.

There have been many debates in our intellectual history, and they have not ended, which hinge on this issue. For the purpose of examining the question let me refer to one of the most celebrated of these, which took place in early nineteenth-century England between Robert Southey and Thomas Babington Macaulay.[3] Southey, then poet laureate, argued that the view of contemporary society as progressing was a complete sham, that life was better in all ways, and especially in the realm of culture, in the sixteenth century of Thomas More. (More, incidentally, had similar complaints about his own age, and wrote *Utopia* to describe a perfect society, thus giving the name that has been worn ever since by this type of political philosophy.) Macaulay rose to the defense of material progress and of individual initiative as its engine. On one point they were in agreement: if men were left free to do what pleased them, the consequence would be emphasis upon the material aspects of individual welfare. For Macaulay this testified to the merits of material welfare, but for Southey it showed that men will act ignobly if left free, thus demonstrating the need for a strong central authority which would be capable of suppressing the materialism of an individualistic society, and would recognize the need to do so.

Southey's argument was as much an attack on individualism as on materialism and continued a line of thought influentially advanced earlier by another great English poet, Samuel Taylor Coleridge. For Coleridge it was plain that society was an organic entity in itself, not merely an aggregation of persons. The "social welfare," in this conception, may be quite different from the welfares of the members of society; indeed, it is implicit in this view that the individual is a factor of production *simpliciter*, his sole role being to contribute to the welfare of an independent entity called "society." There is no way of demonstrating that one ought to regard "social welfare" as an aggregation of individual welfares rather than that of a separate social entity. The only argument that I know which goes beyond a mere dogmatic assertion on this point is as follows: Society may be an organic entity, and the concept of "social welfare" in this sense may be meaningful, but society as such does not possess capacity for articulate speech, so it is necessary that some human organism speak in its behalf. How can one determine whether the "social welfare" so articulated is the true social welfare or merely the preferences of the spokesman? This is not a compelling argument but it is a very strong one, supported by much experience of the unhappy histories of societies which have embraced an organismic social philosophy and its corollary, authoritarian government.

The adoption of an individualistic conception of welfare

is, theoretically, compatible with either markets or state economic planning as mechanisms of economic organization, but conceptions of the Southey type are only compatible with the latter, so this issue bears vitally upon the question of the appropriate scope of governmental action. If the purpose of an economy is to satisfy individual preferences, this can be done by markets or by planning, and the debate in economic terms is an empirical one: which of the two allocates resources most efficiently? But if the purpose of an economy is to satisfy some other aims, then it is clearly not appropriate to rely on the relative prices generated by free markets to govern the allocation of resources since the performances which are to be satisfied reflect a system of values which is fundamentally different from that which lies behind the demand curves of free market transactions. Confusion on this point has greatly muddied the modern debate over economic planning. Some advocates of planning hold a philosophy that is basically individualistic and perceive planning to be more efficient than markets in maximizing individual welfare, but others advocate planning because they reject the meritoriousness of individual preferences. The technical literature on planning tends to suppress this crucial point, conveying the erroneous impression that the debate is solely a matter of positive science rather than fundamental political philosophy.

Obviously, it makes a great deal of difference whether one adopts a view of welfare like that of Southey or like that of Macaulay, but a philosophical individualist need not deny that "cultural" welfare is meaningful and important. The crucial assumption in Southey's argument is that material welfare and cultural welfare are inherently incompatible with one another. If that were so, the individualist would have a difficult case to make, but historical experience provides ample evidence that there is no inherent conflict and, indeed, the two categories of welfare seem to be strongly complementary, if by cultural welfare one does not mean otherworldly concerns, but the accoutrements of civilized life on terra firma, the cultivation of the arts and the promotion of cultural refinement, it is quite clear that these flourish where there are high standards of material welfare. The splendid artistic achievements of Gothic and Renaissance Florence and Venice provide eloquent demonstrations of what can take place in societies where men pursue material riches with prodigious intensity; indeed, even where that effort consists primarily of the bourgeois activity of trade. Material poverty is not a condition of cultural welfare. That economically poor societies have often produced great art is not evidence of their special dedication to higher values; more commonly it indicates the existence within them of a materially wealthy few who can indulge their taste for cultural refinement all the more easily because the labor of others is cheap. Growing material wealth does not erode the taste for cultural welfare, nor is it inimical, in itself, to the servicing of such taste. But if growing wealth is accompanied by decreasing economic inequality, as is often the case, it will raise the relative costs of those goods and services that are labor-intensive, as are many of the things that are requisite to the satisfaction of cultural welfare. The complaint that modern society produces little that compares with the magnificent buildings of the Middle Ages or the furniture of the era of Louis Quatorze does not reflect a decline in taste so much as it evidences decreasing inequality of incomes. If all incomes were equal, who would pay a craftsman to make a fine chair requiring two months of his time?

The plea that governments should be patrons of the arts can be provided with sound economic foundations, but it does not depend upon the proposition that cultural values are eroded by the general growth of material wealth. The argument that material and cultural welfare are not inherently antithetical or empirically incompatible is not, however, an argument that contemporary values are perfect. One cannot even contend that they are "natural," since all men are products of long enculturation, most of which is aimed at the inculcation of values. No proof can be offered for the view that this process must end when the human organism arrives at some age of maturity, after which a pure doctrine of consumer sovereignty should rule as the sole criterion of welfare. Why not continue the process into the adult years? Adults themselves could be better than they are and, moreover, since it is they who are responsible for the enculturation of the young, improvement of the enculturating process can be achieved if one improves the enculturators. The dedicated individualist will immediately see what a pit of snakes opens here. But we cannot avoid it as easily as we can the similar danger that is inherent in the organismic conception of society. One can deny that society is an organism, or question the bona fides of anyone who claims to be its spokesman, but one cannot avoid the fact that man is an altricial animal; that his plastic original potentials are shaped into more definite forms by the actions of others; and that this process does not end with the attainment of adulthood. The demands for goods and services by individuals who seek their private welfares are greatly affected by custom and fashion and are extensively influenced by the activities of educational, cultural, religious and other institutions, and perhaps especially by those of the mass media in both their informational and entertainment functions.

The fact that what people perceive to be useful to themselves cannot be regarded as "pure" or "original" or "natural" wants, which are independent of social and economic processes, poses a serious problem for the doctrine of "consumer sovereignty" as a criterion for the allocation of the limited productive resources available, and opens the door to claims that other criteria are morally, culturally, or politically superior—claims which the individualist finds it difficult to combat. The problem has even seduced some dedicated individualists into a virtual abandonment of their philosophy, as in the celebrated case of John Stuart Mill's argument in *Utilitarianism* that some human pleasures are culturally superior to others, and that some persons are superior judges of this than others. In Mill's defense it should be added that he was aware of the authoritarian snake-pit which this opens, and though romantic idealists like Carlyle and the Comtean positivists rushed to embrace him as a disciple, he refused to be driven by the logic of his own analysis into a political doctrine which he found abhorrent.

Modern economists, with the important exceptions of Frank Knight and J. M. Clark, have devoted little attention to this problem in their efforts to develop the theory of the optimum allocation of resources. But a similar problem has received more notice in their analysis of markets. The point at which a supply curve and demand curve intersect can be regarded as defining the optimum price and output of the commodity or service in question only under certain conditions, one of which is that supply and demand are independent of one another. Tibor Scitovsky has noted that "market exchanges often create not only satisfactions, but also the needs they satisfy, and anything that gives rise to both a need and its satisfaction is of little or no use to anyone."[4] This is rather an extreme statement since it would rule out as worthless a large amount of consumption innovation. To say that a person's welfare is not increased because he had no desire for a digital watch before they appeared on the market would seem to construe welfare in such narrow terms that it would have to be restricted to the satisfaction of little more than basic biological needs. Scitovsky's argument, if carried very far, would even declare much ordinary consumption to be worthless. If a person is calm and content and then is shown a ripe peach, is his welfare not increased by consuming it even though he would have been just as well off if he had not been shown it?

One need not go as far as Scitovsky does, however, to recognize that the principle of consumer sovereignty is not satisfactorily fulfilled when producers are able to generate the demands they serve. This is especially important when a specific producer is linked in this way to a specific consumer, as is the case, to some degree, in the provision of medical services. The patient who goes to a physician does not usually know what it is that he should seek to purchase, and he depends on the physician both to specify the demand for service and to supply it. Some researchers into the economics of medical care have argued that excess capacity never exists in the availability of physicians' services because whenever it threatens to appear, the demand for those services is increased by the physicians themselves through advising their patients to undergo additional treatment. The performance of unnecessary surgery, which one cynic has classified as "remunerectomies," has been frequently noted, even by the medical profession itself. A Canadian medical economist has gone so far as to argue that contrary to widespread opinion, the country already has too many doctors in terms of the ability to supply the "real" needs of patients, and that any increase in the supply of doctors will simply result in an increase in the amount of unnecessary treatment.[5]

There may be other cases too, in which the ability of producers to generate demand undermines the welfare effects of the market system, and one should be wary of the establishment of practices that reduce the independence of the demand and supply sides of the market. The trade in addictive drugs is another clear case in which the independence criterion is not met, and this is a strong argument against the legalization of the trade, since legalization might well increase the ability of suppliers to generate new demands for their products.

The contemporary discussion of demand-supply dependence has however devoted most of its attention to the practice of advertising, which appears to be a potent force in generating demand but does not turn out, upon careful examination, to be of great weight in this respect.[6] The argument, by J. K. Galbraith[7] and numerous others, that advertising is inimical to welfare sometimes seems to be based on the proposition that *anything* that creates a new or additional desire or demand is to be deplored since the utility that is generated by satisfying the desire is merely an assuagement of the disutility that was generated by its creation. If this were so, then human welfare would remain the same if we followed the opposite course, that of reducing our desires and matching this with a reduction in our production of material goods. This could be carried to the point where no demands were served beyond those of biological existence. Advertising is a popular whipping boy, but the conventional wisdom concerning it, as well as being empirically questionable, has served mainly to draw attention away from the important issues: the welfare effects of specific supply-demand interdependencies and the general fact that wants are products of enculturation.

One may recognize that man's wants are not autonomous, however, without being driven to the conclusion that a good society is one in which they are shaped by a central authority according to an expertly designed scheme of enculturation and behavior modification. In the realm of tastes, variety and experimentation is likely to produce better results than order and plan. Human development is nourished best by a rich smörgåsbord of offerings rather than by any single menu, however skillfully designed, and it would be wise to reject any such proposals for bringing order and predictability to this area of human experience regardless of the scientific or ethical credentials that are claimed for them. A few years ago psychologist B. F. Skinner advocated that a scientific program of behavior modification be established to take us "beyond freedom and dignity," which he regarded as insidiously destructive aspirations of contemporary man. To deprive human beings of freedom and dignity is easy; many societies have accomplished it without any assistance from professional psychologists. But if one takes the view that what is needed is more freedom and more dignity, the improvement of taste requires a state of affairs in which cultural leadership is heterogeneous and dispersed, and those who wish to offer recipes of human transformation are permitted freedom to advocate and to inform, but not to coerce.

The discussion up to this point has focused upon man as consumer, demanding goods and services which contribute to his material and cultural welfare through the use he makes of them. But man is also the producer of these goods and services and his welfare is greatly affected by the conditions of his work. This has often been emphasized by academic intellectuals, who, enjoying conditions of work which are nearly paradisaical, sometimes conclude that everyone else must be miserable and alienated. Exaggeration of the point does not destroy its validity, however. Any activity that occupies such a large portion of one's time as work does for a large portion of the population cannot be irrelevant to welfare, and there is no denying the fact that in many occupations the welfare effects of work are purely negative, the activity being undertaken only as a source of income, yielding no direct satisfaction in itself.

The orthodox literature of economics says little about this dimension of welfare that advances much beyond Adam Smith's discussion of compensating wage differentials, and the issue is almost totally absent from theoretical welfare economics. The point is much more prominent in the heterodox literature such as "institutional economics" and Marxian economics and sociology, where the emphasis is most strongly placed upon the influence of work on personality and character, that is, its molding effect upon the plastic human potential. This emphasis is sound since it seems clear that, so far as adults are concerned, their personality characteristics are much more affected by the manner in which they earn their incomes than by how they spend them. Schemes for creating a "new man" invariably focus more on man as producer than consumer. The same pit opens here as was discussed above and, with appropriate variations, the same caveats apply to any such proposals, so I need not repeat them.

The idea that work molds personality is only part of the issue of the welfare effects of the conditions of work, and not the part that is of most prominent immediate concern in democratic societies. Men, *as they are*, seek to avoid negative effects upon their welfares produced by work. The simplest way of accomplishing this is to devote less of one's time to the working role. The shortening of the work week in industrial societies is a response to preferences reflecting in part the disutility of most types of work and the diminishing marginal utility of income as a generator of welfare through consumption. We do not have to resort to the assumption that people are becoming lazy to explain the phenomenon; rational welfare maximization theory does the job better. The individual can do some things by himself to reduce the negative welfare of work, by absenteeism for example, but most of the conditions of work are indivisible conditions and there is little that can be done to satisfy different individual preferences. It is difficult for most enterprises to provide an eight-hour day for one employee and a six-hour day for another, and such difficulties become much greater in respect to other conditions such as the physical environment in which work is performed. As a consequence, the effort to reduce negative welfare effects has become a prominent item of collective bargaining and of state action. We are likely to see a great deal more of such activities in the future.

Indivisibility is a characteristic of many items of consumer welfare as well as producer welfare. In recent years economists and others have devoted a great deal of attention to goods and services that must be consumed collectively and especially to those of them that are provided by governments. It is not certain that the demand for these goods increase greatly as incomes rise; it may be that the demand for them is larger than optimal because of the illusion that they are "free" or because of the greater concentration of their benefits than the taxes that are levied to pay for them; but it is nevertheless quite clear that material and cultural welfare depend to an important extent on the availability of such goods. The state is not the only provider of them, but it has become the dominant institution in the field, partly because it can levy taxes and create money, partly because it possesses sovereign powers more generally, and partly because public goods are believed to achieve redistribution of welfare, which, increasingly, has come to be regarded as a primary duty of the state.

Duration

So far in this discussion we have been examining the dimensions of welfare for a world that is largely timeless and certain. We can unpack the concept of welfare a bit further by considering some of the implications of the fact that the individual life has duration and is exposed to unforseeable hazards.

Students of the distribution of income have often pointed out that the statistical measures that are typically employed for this purpose are deficient because they take no account of changes in a person's income over time. Total lifetime income, if we could measure it, would be better than any single point-of-time income statistic, but as an index of individual welfare it would still be seriously deficient because it would pay no attention to the extent to which the time-pattern of one's income matches the time-pattern of needs. A person who lived in poverty until, on his deathbed, he won the Irish Sweepstakes would have received a larger total income than one who had a steady income of moderate magnitude month by month throughout his lifetime, but no one would argue that his welfare was greater. The same total income generates more welfare when its temporal distribution varies in accordance with need, being relatively low, say, when one is a single youth; taking a sharp temporary rise when a household is formed, since in modern societies this requires considerable capital investment; experiencing another rise when children become expensive; and falling when material needs become less in old age. If life were certain (which would create other problems) and the variation of one's needs predictable, this variation in distribution could be handled by personal financial management, assisted by ordinary market institutions. Some variations in needs *are* predictable and can be serviced in this way, but others are not, so there is some loss of welfare due to temporal maldistribution of income. Distribution among persons will be discussed later in connection with justice, but it is also germane to temporal distribution since if one belongs to a wealthy family, temporal matching of means to needs can be more easily accomplished by interpersonal transfers closely tailored to the circumstances: wedding dowries, gifts, the establishment of educational trusts, etc.

Since a person's welfare is a function of the supply of publicly provided goods that are indivisible, as well as the private goods he purchases for himself, it may also be significantly affected by the number of others with whom he must share their services. This presents no problems if the public sector accommodates its supply of services to changing numbers, but that is not always the case. Difficulties may arise due to variations in the age-distribution of the population, such as are produced by sharp changes in birth rates or immigration rates. A temporary age-cohort bulge is formed by such events and a member of such a cohort will experience crowding in publicly provided facilities that are age-specific: in the schools when one is a youth, in the maternity wards when one is of childbearing age and so on. Persons of equal private income would, on this account, not experience equal levels of welfare.

Temporal maldistributions of this sort are not negligible, but they are not as important as the fact that life is hazardous; one is exposed to the dangers of unemployment, injury and illness, loss of family breadwinner through death or desertion, liability for injury done to others, etc. Perhaps no one would want to make life perfectly certain, but most people are moderate risk-averters and seek by various means to secure themselves against such hazards. To do so requires either the pooling of risks with others, or the accumulation of personal wealth to serve not only as a source of current income, but also as a security cushion against the unexpected. Risk pooling is extensively provided by private enterprise, but one of the most striking developments of recent years has been the entry of the state into this field. This is partly due to the fact that risk pooling is essentially a simple business, requiring little innovative talent, and so can be efficiently managed by clerical administration; partly because some of the hazards are not predictable, even statistically, and protection from them can only be provided by an agency that has taxing and/or money-creating powers; and partly because state-provided insurance has also been viewed as a useful instrument by which to accomplish some interpersonal redistribution of welfare. The last point comes under the heading of justice rather than welfare strictly defined, but at any rate, it is doubtful that this has been as important in the development of such governmental functions as the rise in the general level of incomes. People become more risk-averse when their material standards of welfare rise since they have further to fall from levels to which they have become accustomed, so they buy more protection in private insurance markets, accumulate more wealth to act as a cushion against unexpected or uninsurable hazards, and they also demand more security from the state as part of its public services.

Before ending this discussion of welfare, we must pay some attention to two facts: that societies endure in ways that persons do not, and that social policy operates at a level that is less than the total ecumene. These present some of the most difficult practical problems that must be faced in the promotion of welfare, and the awareness of them has, in modern times, increased very considerably. It is impossible to keep these welfare considerations separated from issues of justice, but all classifications are artificial, and it is more important to examine problems than to keep taxonomies clean.

The individual human life has a definite beginning and a definite end. But the beginnings and ends occur at different calendar dates, so the society which embraces the individuals does not experience the same phenomenon. It endures while the individuals pass, just as a forest endures though individual trees sprout, grow, and die. Some philosophers of history have suggested that societies too have a lifespan but, even if that were so, it would not be germane to the issues we are considering here, since the problem that is created by social duration is not one of preparing for society's maturation, aging, and death, but for its simple persistence or continuation, without such a biological analogue.

In economic terms this means that consideration of the welfare of others—those who will be members of future generations—is unavoiadable. What weight should be attached to the welfare of future generations compared to the present one and what formula is appropriate in making such interpersonal comparisons? For a single individual, considering the different degrees of welfare he might experience at different times of his future life, uncertainty aside, it is rational to apply the ordinary compound interest formula to this problem. Even if he has no personal time preference, the interest rate is one of the price parameters he faces as a decision maker, and he would be irrational to disregard this price, as he would be to neglect any other. But the same reasoning is inapplicable to society's future and there has been a great deal of debate over what is the proper rate of time discount in considering the provisions we should make for the welfare of future generations. In the late nineteenth century, Henry Sidgwick, in his effort to revise utilitarianism as a social philosophy, argued that all persons must be weighted equally, including the yet unborn, so the proper rate of time discount is zero. Some modern socialist writers, considering this problem in the context of economic planning, make a similar argument.

To the extent that the creation of present welfare involves the using up of nonrenewable resources, it is clear that the endowment of future generations is less. If these resources were not substitutable for one another in the production of consumer goods and did not enter into each other's production functions, and if, in addition, we knew when society would come to an end, and the size of its population at each moment of time; then a rational program of exhaustible resource exploitation could be designed following Sidgwick's rule. If society is conceived to be endless, the future population is, in effect, construed to be infinite in size, and Sidgwick's rule drives one to the conclusion that exhaustible resources should not be used *at all*. Similar difficulties are encountered with respect to renewable resources and the problem is further complicated if renewable and nonrenewable natural resources, and nonnatural ones, can act as substitutes for one another in production functions.

It is not possible to establish a clear criterion of what ought to be done in providing for future generations. (It is not even possible to determine quantitatively what *is* done in fact.) Present use reduces the future stock of specific nonrenewable resources (if by the stock we mean that which is in nature, not the *known* stock) but current practices also tend to increase the quantity of physical capital and knowledge (a very potent generator of welfare) and even to create new resources out of hitherto unusable substances. The law of entropy aside, it is not at all clear whether we are running the world down or building it up.

There is, however, one aspect of this problem on which a much less ambiguous judgment can, in my view, be made: the size of future populations. If the relation between per capita output and population size (population being a factor of production as well as constituting the sensors of welfare) is positive, there is a prima facie argument for promoting population growth, but if it is zero or negative, as is probably the case in most countries, the argument for reducing population size is a very strong one. If this were beyond human control there would be nothing to do except sing Malthusian laments, but population size is within human control and can be affected by social policy in powerful ways (some of which, one should note, have important implications for justice and freedom as well as welfare). If one takes an individualistic view, the optimum population is that which maximizes per capita welfare and if that maximum is constant over a range of population sizes, the minimum population which maximizes per capita welfare is the optimum optimorum, since it involves less use of natural resources, less pollution, congestion, etc. If, comparing any two countries, one has a per capita output function which is negative and the other has one which is positive or zero, an argument can be made for moving people from the former to the latter. If this is undesirable for noneconomic reasons, a "second-best" argument can be made for promoting the flow of trade and capital investment between them. If one takes an organismic view of society, however, different conclusions might follow and, of course, if one views the ideal as the maximization of the number of souls singing praises to the creator, the conclusions are clearly very different indeed.

Domain

The issue of migration between societies raises a larger problem, due to the fact that decision-making entities do not embrace the whole of even present humanity. Families, firms, and governments are not ecumenical in the scope of their domains. There is a formal similarity between this problem and the problem of evaluating the welfare claims of future generations, in that there is "social distance" between persons just as there is time distance between generations. One could formulate this too in terms of the discounting formula and say that the welfare of others should be discounted according to the magnitude of the social distance and the rate of social distance discount. Sidgwick's rule implies that one should not discount at all since all persons must be regarded as equal. This rule is applicable within any decision-making entity but not between them. It is arguable that, within a family, the proper rule is to assume that all members are to be considered equal and that, within a state, there should be no discrimination among its citizens. But it is impractical for each of these decision-making entities to apply the rule more widely. If a family were obligated to consider the welfare of others equally with its own members, it could never sit down to dinner with comfort of conscience. Families do discount for social distance (in a subjective way, since there is no natural unit for this distance as there is for time,[8] and no discount rate that is comparable to the market rate of interest) and it is clear that they *must* discount in order to operate at all. The same applies to the state as a decision-making entity. A great deal of the discussion of what should be our obligation to the citizens of other countries is, in effect, an effort to assess the magnitude of social distance between us and them (the degree of cultural similarity, political practices, aspirations for improvement, etc.), and to determine what rate of discount it is proper to apply. However, I am not suggesting here that the vernacular discussion of this problem is so explicit, nor am I suggesting that by formalizing it in this way the door is opened for a technical solution. It is possible that one of the reasons for the modern growth of the state is the view that it is desirable to shift more decisions to entities that are larger in order to reduce the extent of social distance discounting. This, of course, is merely another way of saying that equality is a criterion of justice with growing appeal. This will be discussed further in the next chapter.

The proper domain of welfare can be construed as wider

even than humanity, embracing nonhuman organisms as well. Policies of protecting endangered species are, in effect, based on this conception, when they are not aimed at simply correcting mistakes which man makes in serving his own interests. The idea that other organisms have rights could lead to the application of Sidgwick's rule here too, but it is clearly unworkable. In practice we do discounting here too, at a great variety of rates; we promote the material welfare of pets, dolphins, eagles, and other creatures at some expense to our own, but, in order to combat typhus, we wage unremitting genocidal war on lice, which are no more parasitical than ourselves. Any biological organism that does not possess the capacity to use the energy of sunlight to make sugar is a parasite on other organisms. Occasionally the enthusiasm for "nature" leads social policy to place a premium rather than a discount on the welfare of other creatures, but these are probably transitory extravagances of moral judgment easily corrected by common sense.

Relativity

As a primary good, welfare is more individualistic in nature than justice or freedom. It would be meaningful to speak of the welfare of a solitary person on an island and to examine the factors that effect changes in it, but justice and freedom, as we shall see in the next two chapters, are *social* goods in such a fundamental way that no discussion of them can fruitfully be carried out that does not center upon the relationships of individual persons to one another. However, it is an error (to which the early utilitarian philosophy was prone) to treat the social welfare as a simple aggregation of the separate welfares of individual persons. The welfares of five persons on five isolated islands could, in principle, be added up, but this is irrelevant to the ordinary circumstances of life. At numerous points in this chapter we have had to recognize the socialness of welfare as a primary good and the complexities which this creates. In this final section I want to discuss this issue more directly.

The individualistic utilitarian economist construes the utility of a person to be dependent upon the quantity of goods and services which he has available to satisfy his wants and usually takes a person's income to be a satisfactory quantitative measurement of his aggregate ability to command goods and services. Income, of course, is earned as part of a social activity; some of the goods and services everyone wishes to consume are collective in nature, the preferences people have result in part from their experiences as members of a society, and so on; so it is not possible to regard even the simplest "utility function" of economic theory as immaculately individualistic. But leaving such issues aside, is it correct, as an empirical matter, to depict an individual's utility as dependent solely upon his own income, regardless of the incomes of the other members of his society? If utility has substantive meaning, indicating happiness or degree of satisfaction or something of that sort, even casual observation indicates that the utility of an individual person is affected by his *relative* position in society. All conciliators of labor disputes, for example, are aware of the large role that "differentials" play in industrial relations; grievances multiply when traditional differentials are disturbed, and talk of a strike becomes louder when another group of workers signs a lucrative new contract. Nor is the desire to keep up with the Joneses, or to keep *ahead* of them, confined to a restricted segment of society. Even professors in a school of theology take note of their relative status.

Recognition of such empirical facts requires one to reformulate the utility function of an individual to take into account his status relative to that of the persons he is inclined to compare himself with. In the extreme case, this function could be such that the utility of an individual is *solely* a function of his relative status. In such a state of affairs it may not be possible to increase the utility of the members of society by increased production. If a person's income were doubled or trebled, or multiplied by any positive factor, he would be no happier than before if, at the same time, the incomes of others were increased by the same factor. In such a case, economic progress would seem to be illusory; we would be using productive resources, some of which are nonrenewable, to no apparent purpose. It has recently been argued that this is not an extreme case of purely theoretical interest but is in fact the state in which mankind finds itself, and not only in economically wealthy societies like the United States.[9] The clear implication of this is that further economic growth cannot be justified on the ground that it increases welfare, since it does not.

This appears to be a very disturbing conclusion, at least for the orthodox economist. It seems to say that we now live in a world that is not characterized by scarcity except that which is factitious, a world based solely upon a concern for status and driven by the ignoble sentiment of vanity when one is high and envy when one is low. It is understandable why an economist might be reluctant to accept the verdict that his discipline is no longer relevant, but others might welcome it as an announcement that man has found his way back to the gates of Eden, which will open wide if he could but extirpate the ignoble sentiments from his psyche.

But this argument—that if everyone's personal utility is a function solely of his relative position in society then nothing is gained by a general increase in the quantity of material goods—is less compelling upon careful examination than at first sight. To a degree, it can be regarded merely as a modern variation of an old theme: if happiness consists of fulfilling one's desires, then it can be achieved as well by reducing the desires as by increasing the means to satisfy them. The logic of this is impeccable, so far as it goes. It is difficult to deny that the ascetic who lives on wild plants and possesses no more material goods than he can carry may be as happy as any man. The number of people who are induced by such an argument to follow the ascetic life is small, so the majority of mankind must be irrational, or the logic of the argument must be incomplete. It *is* incomplete in two important ways: it fails to take into account that many of the consequences of human action are unintended by the actors; and its conception of human nature is superficial.

Consider a society that is economically poor, having such limited command over material goods that physical discomfort, illness and disability, and a short lifespan are common. Suppose now that some change takes place which increases that society's material wealth, so that the general level of physical comfort is increased, illness is reduced, and the lifespan is lengthened, but proportionately for all members so that relative positions are unchanged. If empirical analysis of the utility functions of these people revealed that every person's desire is only to raise his *relative* status, would an external observer be compelled to conclude that no improvement had taken place in the society's level of welfare? if a member of this society were to say that he is not happier or more content than before but, nevertheless, he feels that his welfare has been increased, is he being inconsistent or talking nonsense? Considered judgment suggests that such a statement would not be nonsensical and that the external observer's conclusion is erroneous. In this hypothetical illustration it may seem that we have biased the issues by constructing a case where improvements are measurable in objective terms and that this illustration is therefore irrelevant to wealthy societies like modern North America or Western Europe, but this is not the crux of the issue.

In the foregoing hypothetical example I stated vaguely that the improvement of the society's command of material goods was due to "some change." Let us now make this more specific. Suppose that the members of the society, motivated as each one is solely by the desire to improve his *relative* status, devote part of their incomes to capital creation, improve their personal productive abilities, experiment with new methods, engage in invention and innovation, and do other things that increase their economic powers, but that all are equally successful in such efforts; are such activities fruitless? They do not achieve their intended goal since each person's relative status is the same as before, but they have produced an unintended result: general economic improvement. Obviously, it is insufficient to judge the consequences of an action solely in terms of whether it fulfills its intentions. A large part of social science is concerned with analyzing and evaluating the unintended consequences of actions. In economic theory, for example, the merits of competition are judged not in terms of whether each competitor achieves his intended aims, but according to whether the social welfare is increased thereby. Under conditions of perfect competition, every firm tries to make high profits and every one of them fails to do so, but economists do not regard the activity as fruitless. When Adam Smith noted, two centuries ago, that the competing producer serves an end "which was no part of his intention" he directed the notice of social science to its most fundamental task. There is, of course, no law of nature which decrees that all unintended consequences are good. In order to determine whether welfare is served by an action requires not only analysis but the use of some workable criteria of evaluation. The problem which seems to be generated by utility functions in which relative status is the only factor simply reflects an effort to escape from the exceedingly difficult and disquieting burden of making value judgments that cannot be reduced to scientific propositions.

The issue we are here examining goes deeper than we have yet indicated and there are further complexities in the concept of welfare that must be noted. Even if one were to accept the proposition that welfare consists in having what one wants, and could resolve all of the problems so far discussed in this chapter, profound difficulties arise from the fact that one of the things which man appears to want is action itself, and change. He is a discontented animal, unwilling to sit placidly on any optimum. He constantly creates new objectives, not only because his "tastes" have altered, but simply in order to give focus for activity. Much of what he does has little to do with "happiness," and this is not something that has only emerged in modern societies that are economically developed. It has probably been a leading characteristic of human nature ever since man's large forebrain evolved in the early Pleistocene, long before he invented computers or factories, or even agriculture.

If Eden were created anew, and its gates opened to all

comers, the number of people who would take up permanent residence there would be small. Like Aldous Huxley's *Brave New World*, it would be perfect only in the security, predictability, and calmness it would offer, all of which man desires, but only to a degree. Eden would be a nice place to visit but who would want to live there? Only those who do not feel the pains of boredom. The others would cheerfully eat the apple again and depart, or try to make the place habitable by introducing change and uncertainty.

Homo sapiens, as Frank Knight repeatedly emphasized in his writings, is outstandingly the animal that engages in play,[10] the profound philosophical import of which is that the roles of means and ends are interchanged. Goals are set not as ends in themselves but in order to provide focus for activity, which is the true objective. This is plain enough in some athletic pursuits. The object of a basketball game is not to maximize the number of times the ball goes through the hoop; that could be done more effectively by having the ten participants cooperate instead of grouping them into opposing sides. The same transposition of means and ends characterizes a great deal of man's economic activity as a producer of goods and services, so "work" and "play" are not categorically different kinds of activity. The competition of the marketplace serves a function that is at least as fundamental in human nature as man's desire for material improvement: his need to exercise his powers in a world that offers challenge, and even danger.

The impulse to action is not necessarily one that serves the social welfare. Some of its manifestations, such as war and terrorism, are wildly destructive, and one should beware of embracing the romantic notion that the good and the glorious are one. A. O. Hirschman has recently suggested that the growing emphasis upon material or economic aims in the early modern era was supported and promoted by some perceptive philosophers as a way of taming man's passions by diverting them into constructive channels.[11] Samuel Johnson's famous aphorism that "there are few ways in which a man can be more innocently engaged than in getting money" is more majestic than true, contradicted in a hundred respects by economic analysis itself without any assistance from moral philosophy, but there are some inspirations to action that are clearly less innocent than avarice, as evidenced by the miseries they have created over the course of human history. If we were to accept the proposition that since happiness is a matter of relative status there is no point in further economic growth, the consequence might well be that man's impulse to action and his desire for challenge would find their outlets in ways that are inimical to both his material and cultural well-being.

Welfare, as a social good, is clearly an exceedingly complex thing, but a proper appreciation of what is involved in being a *civilized* social animal requires that this complexity be welcomed rather than deplored. Man has achieved great power over nature through his ability to simplify, but he always commits errors, and sometimes great evil, when he attempts to do likewise in his moral and political philosophy.

Three
Justice

THE PROBLEM OF JUSTICE is probably the largest issue in social philosophy, if we measure by the volume of scholarly and public discussion devoted to it, or by the amount of contemporary social policy motivated by it, or by the intensity of feelings which are aroused by it. Justice is the central concern of law and jurisprudence and a large part of the social sciences, and it is also a major one of philosophy, theology, and the arts. Some social philosophies subordinate everything to justice and consider issues of welfare and freedom primarily by reference to it. This is a strong theme which runs through socialist philosophy of both strong and mild variants, as is easily seen by reading Karl Marx, Maurice Dobb, Oscar Lange, A. P. Lerner, R. H. Tawney, Morris Ginsberg, and David Thomson, to mention only a few. But even social philosophies which do not grant such a paramount role to justice have emphasized it increasingly in modern times. Classical liberalism of the last century laid its main emphasis upon freedom, but the social philosophy that is indicated by the modern term "liberalism" (as used in the United States) gives more weight to justice than to freedom, and social philosophers who reserve the central position for freedom have had to coin a new term, "libertarianism," in order to differentiate their point of view.

Justice, like welfare, is an exceedingly complex concept. Unremitting awareness of this is vital, for civilized society is always undermined by the "great simplifiers" and by none more than those who believe that justice is a plain and homogeneous idea. The main object of this chapter is to show some of the complexity of the concept of justice as a social good, in the conviction that we can obtain a better understanding of the way in which the justice criterion has functioned in vernacular politics by emphasizing its variegated nature than by simplification. I will, however, simplify to the extent of focusing the discussion mainly upon issues of an economic nature.

Property

If we use the term "property" in a broad way to refer to any source of income or direct consumption utility, we may consider the issue of justice as having to do with the justification of property ownership. there are three main questions that are involved here: (1) What kinds of procedures which lead to the *acquisition* of property can be considered just? (2) What procedures by which persons *transform* one kind of property into another are just? (3) Is the *distribution* of property that results from just procedures of acquisition and transformation automatically just, or are there criteria that may validly be employed to evaluate the justness of that distribution as such?

In John Locke's second *Treatise of Civil Government* (1689), which has had an enormous and enduring impact on Western political philosophy, the argument is made that a man justly owns what he has "removed from the state of nature" by his labor. This seems quite straightforward, but even if we attempt to apply this principle to the acquisition of land in a hitherto unpopulated territory, difficulties arise. Does one acquire land merely by walking over it or is the "labor" involved something more than that and, if so, what? If one puts a fence around an area, is the area enclosed thereby one's property, or does ownership apply only to that part of it on which the fence rests? And so on. Further difficulties arise, as Locke himself noted, when there is no longer any unoccupied land, and they multiply very considerably when one considers property that is acquired by a process involving division of labor. What portion of a finished automobile is the just property of a particular assembly line worker? Further: can a just property right be acquired by inheritance? If not, then the previous owner of the property did not have unrestricted rights to it because he could not dispose of it as he wished. But if one person has a right to bequeath his property to another, then presumably the latter has a right to regard such property, acquired without labor or effort, as his own. Is a sum of money won in a lottery justly acquired? Money, found by chance on the street, which is untraceable? If stealing is unjust, is it also unjust to steal from a thief and if so, to whom is the injustice done? And so on. These are difficult questions to answer, but we have laws, reflecting social policy, concerning all of them: homestead laws, wage-contract laws, inheritance laws (and taxes), gambling laws, laws governing the ownership of findings, and laws governing stolen property.

Property is "transformed" from one form to another by trading in markets. Prevalent market prices determine how much of one type of property can be obtained for property of another type. What determines whether the system of prices is just? Is it just if there is perfect competition and all prices are parametric so far as the individual trader is concerned, no one being able to affect any price by his own actions? A great deal of modern economic theory appears to assume this to be the case and some economists have made explicit statements to this effect. Is a transaction just if it involves a deferred payment and, during the period of deferral, a change takes place in the value of the contract's unit of account? Many people think that inflation is unjust in this sense. Would the matter be different if the inflation had been anticipated by the parties in setting the terms of the contract? Some transactions involve pooling, such as in insurance contracts. Is it just to discriminate in such pooling by, for example, offering professors lower life insurance rates than coal miners, or does justice require that those exposed to low risks pool with those exposed to high ones? Is it proper to differentiate between men and women in the determination of annuity rates on the statistical ground that women on the average live longer than men, or does this constitute improper sexual discrimination?

Some recent writers on fundamental political philosophy (e.g., Robert Nozick and James Buchanan) have argued that justice consists in the working of just procedures without regard to the end results they produce. Most people would reject this, I think; at any rate I would.[1] If the procedures by which property is acquired and transformed are just, but they result in gross inequalities of income, or incomes for some that are below the needs of existence, are we bound to regard that distribution as just and not legitimately alterable by state action? On the other hand, should we look solely at the end results? Most people would not regard the distribution of property (or income) as speaking plainly for itself as to its justice without reference to why it is what it is. If all the poor were lazy it would seem to call for a different ethical judgment, and a different social policy, than if all the poor were physically disabled.

Various modern writers on property have recognized that property ownership under any legal system never confers an unlimited right to use it as one wishes, but rather that it is always a bundle of rights and restrictions, permitting a person to do some things with his property and not others. Recognition that this is not merely the nature of the property right under actual laws, but, inescapably, a characteristic of any property right that can be philosophically defined, introduces the necessary recognition of complexity into the discussion of property. Nevertheless, some order can be imposed on this complexity by regarding the right of property as an aspect of the broader question of justice and attempting to throw light on the latter concept by unpacking it. A useful place to begin is with an oft-quoted passage from David Hume who perceived, with his customary clarity, the most essential feature of the problem of justice, and especially its connection with economics:

> If men were supplied with everything in the same abundance [as air and water], or if *every one* had the same affection and tender regard for *every one* as for himself, justice and injustice would be equally unknown among mankind.
>
> Here then is a proposition, which, I think, may be regarded as certain, *that 'tis only from the selfishness and confined generosity of men, along with the scanty provision nature has made for his wants, that justice derives its origin.*[2]

Note that Hume does not say that a society of unconstrained plenty, or one in which every person was benevolent, would be a just society. He says, more correctly, that under either of these conditions, both justice and injustice would be "unknown," that is, the concepts would be literally meaningless. This is a point of crucial importance; it forces to our attention the perception that the problem of justice derives from the condition of *conflict*. From Plato, through Sir Thomas More, to B. F. Skinner, men have dreamed of societies of transcendent merit which have gone beyond scarcity, beyond ambition, beyond the desire even for freedom and dignity, beyond, that is to say, everything that creates conflict among men. These ideal societies are usually described as just ones but, as Hume's remark makes plain, they are so only in the sense that "justice" would be a meaningless concept in them. Any inhabitant of such a society who used that term would only be making a noise with his vocal apparatus. The real task of a theory of justice, therefore, is not to describe how to render the concept empty by *eliminating* conflict, but to find rules that can be used to *mediate* it.

The long history of utopianism, and the powerful attraction such efforts still have on some minds, shows the depth of man's concern for justice even though utopianism is a misguided approach to the problem. Short of full utopian reconstructions, this concern is also demonstrated by the great appeal of simple rules of just conduct at the personal level. "Do unto others as you would have them do unto you;" "treat others as ends and not as means;" "act only in such ways that your action could be a universal rule"—these are a few of the simple formulas that have won wide approval. But it is easy to undermine such simplicities. G. B. Shaw once pointed out that one should *not* do to others as you would have them do unto you because they may have different preferences; the treatment of other men as means as well as ends is unavoidable in an economy of specialization; there are very few actions, and those of little consequence, that can be universalized according to the Kantian rule; and so it goes for every simple formula that has been (or can be) devised.[3]

In the older philosophical and theological literature, a distinction is often made between commutative justice and distributive justice. The former is essentially a proceduralist conception which ascribes qualities of justice to end results solely on the ground that they are the consequences of a procedure that is inherently just. Distributive justice focuses upon the characteristics of the end results themselves. Commutative justice is sometimes regarded as served when the procedure constitutes an exchange of physical equivalents as, for example, in the Old Testament rule of "an eye for an eye and a tooth for a tooth," or in the provision of the Code of Hammurabi (c.2100 B.C.) that if a member of a family is murdered, then an equivalent member of the murderer's family, not necessarily himself, must be done to death. The desire for revenge still can be found in individual utility functions and retribution may be a principle of justice of some power in the vernacular, and in other circles, but this procedure is clearly a negative-sum game and has little relevance to economic matters. There would be no point even in exchanging a shirt for an identical shirt, so the principle of commutative justice requires specification that is much more complex than the Old Testament maxim.

Fair Exchange

Adam Smith's greatest contribution to the study of social phenomena was his perception of the possibility of spontaneous order which, while not dispensing altogether with the need for law and custom as order-producing constraints, demonstrated that a Hobbesian sovereign is unnecessary. Smith's spontaneous order is one that is produced by the mechanism of markets; that is, by voluntary exchange. Since Smith's day, this has been the basic analytical paradigm of orthodox economic theory.

The exchange paradigm has not been confined to economics, however. All social scientists and social philosophers who view social behavior as reflecting the rational pursuit of individual self-interest make extensive use of it. This is evidenced in the recent efforts, especially by Nozick and Buchanan, to construct contractarian political philosophies, and in the modern theory of collective choice. Sociological theory has tended to emphasize the nonindividualistic and the nonrational aspects of human behavior, but in that discipline too there has been an important school of thought, represented by Georg Simmel, Sir James Frazer, and Bronislaw Malinowski, and more recently by James S. Coleman, G. C. Homans, and P. M. Blau, which has emphasized the exchange nature of social interaction, regarding it as encompassing not only the more strictly economic aspects of life, but also its religious, cultural, customary, and even its intellectual ones as well.[4]

It is evident then, that exchange is a central concept of modern social thought. It is not confined to the positive analysis of social behavior either; a strong theme in ethical literature, and in vernacular discussion, is that social and economic relationships are just when they are characterized by voluntary exchange. This joins the concept of justice to that of freedom (as well as welfare), which gives it exceptionally strong appeal. The key word "voluntary" in this formulation is, however, difficult to define. In economic theory the construction that is placed upon it emphasizes the necessity for the existence of alternative opportunities: an exchange is voluntary, and just, when each of the parties has many potential exchange partners. The analysis of perfect competition is a tool for examining real markets, but it also reflects a justice principle, which we can call the idea of "fair exchange." The view that monopoly is unjust is based mainly on this idea. The special attention paid to public goods also stems partly from the recognition that alternative suppliers are few and the exchange process is characterized by coercion.

Another element that is essential to the conception of a free market process as constituting fair exchange is that the parties must have true information concerning the characteristics of the things exchanged, and the terms of the transaction. Fraudulent practices obviously are not irrelevant to justice, nor to economic efficiency for that matter. Some further insight into this aspect of fair exchange is provided if we think of it in terms of expectation: for example, fraud may be considered as unfair because it leads to the disappointment of legitimate expectations. The basic idea that is involved here is the general ethical principle that a promise is a moral obligation or, looked at the other way around, that the recipient of a promise has a moral right to the fulfillment of the expectations that are generated by the promise. This is a very strong idea of justice in the vernacular. On the personal level it is striking how annoyed, and righteously annoyed, people become when promises are broken. Say to a man that you will give him a hundred dollars on Friday and if you do not, he will be angry even if there is no other reason why you are obligated to pay him the sum. The breaking of a promise is even regarded by some persons as legitimizing unjust acts, or even mean and vicious ones. Similar sentiments can be generated by promises of a more general and/or social nature.

More broadly, the existence of expectations serves as the foundation of prescriptive claims, the argument being that when a status or a practice has persisted for some time, people have been led to expect that it will continue and have acquired a right to its continuance. This is usually argued in terms of direct relations among individuals (as, for example in the case of squatters' rights or the right to a customary roadway); but if we consider that a society gives an implied promise to its members, by means of the duration or persistence of a practice, that it will continue, we arrive at one of the fundamental doctrines of political conservatism.

Applications of this principle are present in many modern discussions of social policy, often advocated by people who do not regard themselves as conservatives in political philosophy. A specific application of exceptional current importance is worth noting—the problem of *inflation*. Reading the popular literature impresses one with the extent to which inflation is regarded as a problem that is not merely economic but moral; at any rate, it is invested with more moral rhetoric than one finds in discussion of most other economic problems. Below the clichés, there resides the view that an economic system in which exchanges and debts are made and settled in fiat money creates the expectation that the real value of the money will not alter. Inflation is immoral because it disappoints this legitimate expectation. The argument that inflation as an economic problem must be given priority over other economic problems is technically arguable, but the priority which it has in fact been given in the economic policies of many countries does not derive from economic analysis so much as it does from the moral elements that adhere to the issue, stemming from the ethical principle that promises, even implied ones, should be kept, as one of the conditions of fair exchange.

The idea of justice as fair exchange is, however, incomplete, not only because certain things, such as public goods, *cannot* be exchanged under the requisite conditions, but also because it is widely held that there are things that *ought* not to be objects of exchange at all. Primary among them are political and judicial office and similar things that are intimately connected with the operation of the basic social framework.[5] Democratic political philosophy holds that offices should be open to all (equality of opportunity), that the ultimate counters of political power (votes) should be distributed equally, and that the sale of both offices and votes should be prohibited. The specification of prohibited exchange is not restricted to such things however. The sale of injurious substances that are strongly habit-forming is usually prohibited even when information concerning these characteristics is widely known. Some societies extend such prohibitions to things that are regarded as morally damaging, such as sexual services, and some to ones that are viewed as offending religious rules, such as the consumption of pork or alcohol. Obviously, the principle that some things are not legitimate objects of market exchange can be extended very far, opening the door to paternalistic government, but even a strict construction of the view that justice consists of fair exchange cannot be complete.

All justice ideas other than fair exchange are more distributive than commutative in character, focusing mainly upon the ethical quality of end results rather than upon the ethical quality of procedures in themselves. Four such ideas can be usefully distinguished: *desert, equality, equality of opportunity,* and *need.* These will be discussed below.

Desert

The idea of desert has a wide variety of meanings. One may say, for example, that a person is deserving because of his personal character; or because of the status characteristics of some position that he occupies; or one may say that he is deserving due to the performance of certain especially meritorious acts; or because he has hitherto been a victim of misfortune; or we may focus upon his work, saying that he is deserving because he works diligently or because the work itself is arduous or dangerous or is especially valuable in some way. All of these are meaningful statements and can be found in both vernacular and scholarly discussions of justice. They are, however, clearly quite different in their implications so far as distributive justice is concerned.

Aristotle, in the *Nichomachean Ethics,* contends that the proper basis of distrubutive justice is desert, which he took to be derived from merit. In a just society each man receives, relative to others, in accordance with his relative merit. Aristotle was not, however, able to advance this argument by explaining how relative merits are to be ascertained, and acknowledged that what is regarded as meritorious may be quite different in different societies. This argument, if joined to Aristotle's metaphysical essentialism, could easily be made into a defense of that often quoted banality of America's Gilded Age: "Why should they have the lion's share? . . . [Because] the lion's share belongs to the lion."[6] In early Protestant theology, much emphasis was placed on absolute personal merit, no consideration of relativity being necessary since rewards would be paid in Heaven, where there is no scarcity. In John Calvin's view the quantum of a person's merit as a soul is fixed in the zygote and there is no way of either depreciating it or adding to it by worldly acts; but that did not prevent his followers from making the 180 degree turn that was necessary to orient behavior to the pursuit of worldly wealth. Martin Luther construed merit to be earned by labor, which opened the door more directly to worldly ambition.

The advice of Christ to the rich man seeking eternal life to "give all that thou hast and distribute unto the poor" implies that, while the recipients might benefit, the donor does as well, since charity earns merit—an early anticipation of the powerful comfort provided by the Pareto criterion. If the system of rewards transcends the mundane world, justice can be construed as nondistributional—desert that finds its reward in Heaven presents no economic problems. But Christ's injunction, when regarded in mundane terms, poses difficulties. It fuses the justice conceptions of desert and equality or, at least, it has no equilibrium point short of perfect equality, if all those who are relatively rich are to follow it without limit. But in vernacular discourse the more common theme of desert due to personal merit is antiegalitarian, a just society being construed as one that places the meritorious person in a superior status relative to others. This does not necessarily call for *economic* inequality; deservingness can be recognized by medals, citations, honorary degrees, testimonial dinners, engraved watches, and all sorts of things. Some societies have placed great stress on noneconomic recognitions of merit, but in a materialistic civilization they seem to fall flat (perhaps because their low marginal cost leads to excessive supply), so the prizes that are highly valued involve large checks in small envelopes, as Alfred Nobel recognized when he established the most prestigious of the world's awards.

A full examination of desert as a criterion of justice would be very lengthy and lead one far away from considerations that are of practical import for modern social policy and the role of government. From this more restricted standpoint, the most important idea is that deservingness is proportional to contribution; that what one should get in determined by what one produces. As an ethical principle, this is closely connected with the commutative justice criterion of fair exchange, previously discussed.

In a simple society of individual self-sufficiency, the contribution criterion of desert would be, in a sense, automatic. Each person's productive activity would contribute only to his own welfare and he would deserve to keep whatever he produces. The criterion would operate to condemn theft, but that is all. In a society of division of labor and exchange, it is no longer plain what each person produces or what the "true value" of that production is. His productive activity is a contribution to a collective output and it becomes difficult to determine what part of this he deserves to receive. This problem is addressed in a penetrating way by the theory of marginal productivity. We may identify a person's contribution as being the value that his effort *adds* to the collective output. When it was shown by P. H. Wicksteed in 1894 that the sum of these marginal products would exactly equal the total product (under certain assumptions), some economists felt that they had hold of a proposition that was not only scientifically elegant but that solved the age-old problem of the ethics of distribution. The leading American economist of that time, J. B. Clark, was especially enthusiastic about the philosophic possibilities of the "marginal productivity theory of distribution," as it was called. The leading sociologist, W. G. Sumner, was even more certain that the problem had been solved by the economists. As a principle of economic justice, however, marginal productivity theory has some severe difficulties. Not only does it neglect other justice criteria such as need (the marginal product of a disabled person, for example, is zero), equality, etc., but it has difficulties of its own, as follows:

(1) The marginal productivity theorem applies only to a static economy; in a dynamic one the sum of the marginal products does not equal the total output and there are residual products (which may be negative) whose ownership is undetermined.

(2) The marginal product of any factor depends on the quantity of other factors that are complementary to or substitutional with it in the productive process. In order to argue that a man gets what he deserves when he receives his marginal product, one must accept the fact that this marginal product is not uniquely determined by his own efforts. Some would accept this as a condition of deservingness but others would not.

(3) The marginal productivity of a factor is not its *physical* output, but its addition to the *value* output, so it depends in part on the market price of the product produced. But this, in turn, depends in part on the distribution of income. So, the prior distribution of income must itself be justified before we can employ marginal productivity theory as a justification of the distribution of income—a rather nasty circularity.

(4) The theorem necessarily ascribes marginal produc-

tivity to all factors of production, human and nonhuman, but only humans receive income. If, for illustrative purposes, we consider two factors of production, "labor" and "property," then the income of a person is the sum of his receipts from the sale of whatever quantity of labor and property services he owns. For any particular person, Income $= MP_L \cdot L + MP_P \cdot P$, where L and P are his quantities of labor and property and the MPs are their marginal products. Even if everyone had the same quantity of labor to dispose of and the prices of labor and property services were equal to their marginal products, a justification of the distribution of property ownership would be a necessary condition of the proposition than the resulting distribution of income is just. Needless to say, the issue of property ownership has been a major focus of the continuing debate on the ethics of distribution.

(5) If a factor of production is fixed in aggregate supply, an increase in the demand for it will raise its value marginal product and hence its price, but can it be said that the owners of that factor deserve the higher reward? Are they not merely the fortunate possessors of a type of monopoly? The rate of return for the factor is not a "necessary" supply price since the aggregate supply would be the same at a lower rate. Long before the formal development of marginal productivity theory, this consideration was the basis of an attack on the contribution-desert criterion of distributive justice engendered by the Ricardian theory of rent. Together with (4) above, it was the foundation of a wide variety of reformist and radical argument, including various proposals for the nationalization of land, the single-tax movement of Henry George, and the basic philosophy of the Fabian Society and the early British Labour party. The initial argument along these lines was seemingly undermined by the realiza-

tion of later economists that rent was not a special category of distribution but merely the marginal product of land, but this did not serve to restore the contribution-desert criterion of justice since the inelasticity of supply was not thereby made irrelevant to the issue. Instead, the scope of the objection was greatly enlarged at about the same time by recognition of the fact that land was not unique in this respect in either the short run or the long, and, accordingly, there may be a rent component in many other sources of income. In a world where rewards reflect desert, and desert is determined by marginal product, one would be fortunate if endowed by genetics, or by property inheritance, or simply by the slowness of supply responses, with factors that were commonly scarce and in high demand.

These various difficulties weaken any claim that may be made that marginal productivity supplies an adequate principle of distributive justice, even if desert alone, and desert construed as springing from contribution, were acceptable as the sole foundation of such a principle.[7]

Equality

"Equality" is one of the most ambiguous words in our language, which is paradoxical in view of the fact that it implies perfect precision. Equality means equation; we write an equation sign and put something on one side and something else on the other, and declare them to be equal. But in order to do this properly one must specify clearly *what entities* are being placed on either side of the equation sign, and in respect of *what dimension* their equality is asserted or measured. A great deal of the literature on equality proceeds in blithe disregard of these requirements, especially in mathematical welfare economics since abstract symbols do not seem to require such specifications.

A characteristic of much religious thought is that it asserts the equality of *all men* as entities, which seems to be quite unambiguous, until one probes whether infants, madmen, heretics, and servants of Satan are included. On the dimensional issue there is great room for differences of specification also. Luther argued that all men are equal in respect of possessing capacity (although not necessarily *equal* capacity) for spiritual understanding, but Calvin argued that all men are equal in being depraved (again, not necessarily to the same degree). Jacob Viner, in his Jayne Lectures, complained that one of the most prevalent errors of modern thought is the perception that religion has typically been egalitarian in its view of men.[8] Viner pointed out that, to the extent that this is true at all, such egalitarianism is confined to the other world. He might have added that even there, the egalitarianism consists primarily of common subordination to authority, like Hobbes' view of the equality that reigns in the earthly polity of dictatorship. The origin of a more useful concept of equality probably lies in jurisprudence, since it seems rather pointless to go through a procedure to determine guilt or innocence without holding, at least as the ideal, that the quality of evidence is independent of whose side it bears on, so the parties are equal in this respect. From this source, it began to work its way into politics in the eighteenth century and into economics in the nineteenth.

Still, the problem of what entities are to appear on either side of the equation sign in a satisfactory concept of equality is not easy to solve. Leaving lunatics and other anomalies aside, it is not clear for example whether the entities should be individuals or families. If the former, then any measure of the degree of inequality of income would not serve as an adequate measure of inequality of welfare since it would neglect economies of household production and the capture of positive externalities that are uniquely possible in such an organization. If the family is chosen as the entity we encounter difficulties of definition. Do homosexuals living together constitute a family? Do in-laws who share kitchens and bathrooms and nothing else constitute one family or two? Is a commune of two hundred persons one big family? Moreover, if the family were truly regarded as the entity, there would be very slender grounds for taxing inheritances since families do not die when individuals do. An egalitarian who is unwilling to embrace this conclusion may find himself driven to the adoption of an even more individualistic position than many of his conservative opponents.

The degree of inequality, as measured by one of the standard devices such as the Gini Coefficient, would be much greater if individuals were considered as the measurement entities rather than families. A great many individuals such as children and housewives have no explicit incomes of their own, so there would be a great concentration of entities at the zero end of the income scale, making the measurement of inequality very high. The magnitude of the coefficient of inequality would be affected by fluctuations in birth rates, which produce alterations in the age distribution of the population. An increase in birth rates would result in a rising inequality coefficient for eighteen years or so, and than a fall, simply because of the change in the number of entities with zero income. Perhaps no one would object to a deviation from pure individualism to the extent of restricting the definition of entities to persons over a certain age, say eighteen, but this would only mitigate the problem somewhat since, even among adults, it is characteristic of most societies that incomes vary with age. Wages and salaries typically rise with age, as does property income also, on account of both personal accumulation and inheritance. The effect of this is that a rise in birth rates will result, some eighteen or so years later, in a rise in the coefficient of inequality as new adults begin their earning careers low on the income ladder; a decade or so later, the coefficient will fall as these persons come into the middle income ranges.

This difficulty has recently been the focus of intense discussion in the economic literature, initiated specifically by a proposal by Morton Paglin that inequality of income should be measured *within* age-groups.[9] By this procedure, individuals are compared only with others of the same age-group and the aggregate coefficient of inequality is constructed by combining such age-constant coefficients. If one proceeds in this way, Paglin shows that the degree of income inequality has fallen substantially over the past thirty years; whereas if no account is taken of the change in age distribution the degree of inequality has been pretty much constant.

There is no doubt that inequality measurements can be greatly affected by age-distribution changes, but it does not follow that the proper measurement is one which eliminates such influences. Why should one be interested only in inequality among persons of the same age and not in differences among persons of different ages? If income comparisons are restricted to persons of the same age, why not restrict them also to persons of the same sex, race, educational background, and other characteristics? Moreover, why restrict the measurement to persons who share the characteristic of belonging to the same nation? If we were to measure income inequality by comparing Alabamians only with Alabamians, Coloradians with Coloradians and so on, the degree of inequality in the United States would be different than if we compared Americans generally with Americans, and this, in turn, would be different than if we were to extend the scope of comparison beyond the nation to the world at large. So, it is apparent that even if we choose to regard adult individuals as the proper entities for income inequality studies, there still remain a host of difficulties in entity definition which can be met only by compiling many measurements of inequality rather than one, and by using different measurements, as appropriate, to throw light on different aspects of inequality.

Entity definition is not the only problem that must be faced in an empirical examination of this issue. Even if we could determine what entities are to be placed on opposite sides of the equality—or inequality—sign, it is not certain what dimension of the entities should be measured. In comparing two persons, we might measure their weight, height, "scholastic aptitudes" and innumerable other dimensions. The economic statistics on this matter take it for granted that personal income, or wealth, are the appropriate dimensions. Strong arguments can be made for use of these as indicators of a person's ability to command the employment of productive resources to serve his material wants, but such use is far from perfect in this respect since a large number of important goods are not provided by the market sector of the economy and we should have to supplement such measures, as some economists have tried to do, by calculating the distribution of the benefits of publicly provided services such as defense, foreign policy, roads and streets, etc. If we were to insist on the hard specification of equality that is required by a literal interpretation of the equation sign, economic equality would be observable only under highly exceptional circumstances. If two prisoners of war receive identical Red Cross parcels, we could say that they were equal in the sense of material possessions. If they trade, exchanging chocolate for aspirin say, even this measurement breaks down, and one would have to resort to some criterion of justice other than equality to justify their engaging in such practices.

The equality criterion is one that judges the merit of an end-state of affairs, but such things as money income or Red Cross parcels are means more clearly than they are ends. If, recognizing this, one adopts the view that the proper dimension of measurement is welfare, then additional elements of great difficulty are inserted into the analysis of distributional equity. A person who suffers from a physical disability say, has needs that require that he receive more income if his welfare is to be made equal to that of a person who has no such disability. So equalization of welfare requires inequality of income because of such differential needs. This argument is a compelling one when viewed as a rejection of the claim that equality of income can serve as the sole criterion of justice, but it is not free of difficulties of its own when viewed as a substitute sole criterion. The most obvious problem is that this approach focuses on a dimension that is not observable. The difficulty of measuring inequality of income may be a technical one and therefore potentially surmountable, but it is apparent that one can never measure welfare, or happiness, or contentment, so equality is preserved as the sole criterion of justice only at the expense of making it impossible to determine empirically which of any two states of affairs is the more equal. A greater difficulty, from the philosophical standpoint, is that it opens the door to the general proposition that people differ in their ability to extract welfare from income. If one person needs more income than others because he is disabled, why does another not need more because he has an exceptionally saturnine, woebegone, or melancholy disposition? Common observation shows that some people are made happy by very little while others are still unhappy when they have very much. What about people who are only made happy by superior status, i.e., those whose utility functions contain *relative* incomes as powerful arguments? Or, what about those who prefer subservience to others? As someone has noted, one could construct an ideal society composed of sadists and masochists by simply matching complementary preferences. The welfare egalitarian would have to argue that some things that make utility functions nonidentical are legitimate and others are not, but once having abandoned his basic proposition, which is that those functions must be construed as identical, it is not easy to prevent a total erosion of the egalitarian position. (This problem was discussed more fully in the previous chapter on welfare.) It seems better to handle the problem of the special claims of the needy by accepting need as a separate criterion of justice rather than as an aspect of equality.

In the economic literature the dominant critique of distributional equality is not that it conflicts with other justice criteria but that, as a practical matter, it conflicts with the aim of economic efficiency—the use of scarce resources to generate the output from which all the distributive shares are drawn. If everyone received equal rewards it would seem rational to minimize the amount of work, or at least those conditions of work that generate negative personal welfare.

Equality could only function in an Edenic state where all work is a pleasure or where there is no necessity for it.[10] Some thinkers have sought to resolve this problem by subordinating justice to efficiency;[11] others, ever hopeful of the capacity of technical contrivances to solve moral problems, have aimed at inventing devices which insulate the distribution system and the production system from one another;[12] but the main theme of welfare economics, since Sidgwick and Pigou, is that distributional equity is an insoluble difficulty that must be coped with by other (i.e., political) means.

In many countries, the search for greater equality has focused not upon income or the various means to acquire it, but upon a specific kind of productive property: property in land. This has deep historical roots, going back to the feudal age when land was virtually the only source of political power and social status as well as income. When the desire for greater equality in land ownership is extended to the modern economy, the conflict between equality and efficiency may become exceptionally severe. In Mexico, for example, a large proportion of the labor force is engaged in agriculture, but agriculture produces a much smaller proportion of the total output of the economy. Moreover, within agriculture itself, a large part of the output is produced by a much smaller proportion of the agricultural labor force, that which is employed on the larger, more efficient, farms. Yet many Mexicans see their hope for economic improvement to lie in redistribution of the land and this has become a potent political issue in that country. If the land were redistributed, there would indeed be greater equality of land ownership and perhaps greater equality of income and wealth more generally, but it would almost certainly be achieved at the expense of a substantial decline in the per capita output of the economy since the labor force would be reallocated from more productive activities to less productive ones. The conflict between justice and welfare becomes especially serious therefore when equality as a justice criterion is aimed at the distribution of a specific factor of production which is limited in aggregate supply, such as land. Specific egalitarianism is likely to be much less inimical to welfare when it is focused instead upon the distribution of the output of consumer goods. The sentiment that certain goods should be distributed more equally than general income can be accommodated, if properly done, without encroaching unduly upon efficiency.[13] This is a problem that comes more properly under the heading of need, which is discussed in the concluding section of this chapter, rather than that of equality.

Equality of Opportunity

So far the criterion of equality has been examined in terms of a characteristic that could be observed in a certain end-state such as the distribution of income. There is also a strong strain of thought which focuses instead upon equality of opportunity as a justice criterion. This is an alternative to equality but, in certain respects, it also goes beyond it. If one could meet all the difficulties recorded above, arriving at satisfactory specifications of the entity, and the criterion dimension, and also define the optimum degree of inequality (not being zero), an ethical observer might still be dissatisfied with a state of affairs that was recorded to be at the optimum. If, for example, further study disclosed that, say, in successive generations, all the persons relatively high in the later distributions were children of those who occupied the same relative positions in earlier ones, one might well conclude that the justice of the system was palpably incomplete. Without more faith than is warranted in the genetic transmission of ability, the conclusion would be inescapable that the persisting optimum degree of inequality merely represented the establishment of a hard hierarchical order.

The idea of equality of opportunity rather than equality of results has been strongly advocated by some social philosophers, and it is the justice concept that lies behind such social policies as the prohibition of racial and other discrimination and the financing of education from public funds. Not many would argue that these are not desirable social policies or that the criterion of equality of opportunity is ethically invalid. There are some, indeed, who defend it as the paramount criterion of justice or even as the paramount social good. The idea has been and will continue to be a touchstone of social policy, which justifiably has great appeal, but also is not without ambiguity. A. M. MacLeod has recently demonstrated this with compelling force.[14] He points out that the word "opportunity" must necessarily mean opportunity to do something, or become something, or obtain something, etc.; the phrase "equality of opportunity" is empty without such specification. There may, however, be many such specifications, referring, for example, to educational opportunity, occupational opportunity, opportunity for self-fulfillment, etc., and it is not obvious which of these should be the object of policy. This would be a minor difficulty if these various forms of opportunity were independent of, or complementary to, one another; but if they are not, it means that one can only obtain a greater opportunity of one sort by sacrificing some of another sort, and there would seem to be no way in which the optimum mixture of opportunities can be specified.

MacLeod points out also that the term "opportunity" not only requires specification but is subject to ambiguity in itself. To say that John Smith has an opportunity to achieve a state X may mean that it is entirely up to him whether he achieves X or not; but it is normally the case that if Smith wants to achieve the state X it is necessary that he do the action Y. Doing Y, however, may not guarantee that X will ensue. For example, if Smith wishes to be a lottery winner he must buy a ticket, but buying a ticket will not assure that he will become a winner; it is necessary, but not sufficient. Analogies with education and occupational opportunities are plain. If a person wishes to become a physician he must be admitted to a medical school, but such admission is not normally sufficient to assure that he will become a physician. So the only thing that is provided by equality of opportunity is that everyone has a *chance* to do or become what he wishes. If one were to argue that all chances must be equal for there to be equality of opportunity, one would be saying that a world of equal opportunity is one in which all have equal chances to become physicians, concert pianists, movie actors, etc., irrespective of physical endowments and talents. Since this is clearly unworkable, it becomes necessary to redefine equality of opportunity to mean that the opportunity is open, not to all, but to those *capable* of achieving the desired state; which amounts to saying that no inappropriate or irrelevant criteria must be in force such as, for example, the color of a person's skin. This is the basis of antidiscrimination policy and it is clearly an ethical principal of outstanding merit, but, as MacLeod points out, it is not always easy to determine what are inappropriate or irrelevant criteria.

Some people have argued, for example, that if it can be demonstrated that the average I.Q. of blacks is lower than that of whites this is a valid basis for practicing racial discrimination in education. Leaving aside the doubts that any careful scientist must entertain concerning the adequacy of I.Q. measures, are the policy implications of such data clear? William Shockley argues that the implication is that whites should have more education than blacks, but R. H. Tawney would contend that the reverse is obligatory: that education should be used to compensate for other deficiencies. My own position on this matter is that average I.Q. statistics, even if they were sound in themselves as indications of learning ability, are totally irrelevant in this connection. Even if the *average* I.Q. of blacks were lower than that of whites, there would be many blacks with higher I.Q.s than many whites, and a policy of selecting students by their I.Q.s, whether it is done for Shockley's reasons or for Tawney's, would only be efficient if it were color-blind. This, it seems to me, is a relatively easy case, but one should not expect to find that all problems of determining what discrimination is appropriate and what is inappropriate are so straightforward; and perhaps even this case is only straightforward *to me*, since contemporary policy seems to be based on racial discrimination, which is supported by many who advocate equality of opportunity.

Even in cases where the reduction of a certain kind of discrimination would clearly increase equality of individual opportunity, it does not necessarily follow that one should do so. There may be other objectives that are considered to be superior to equality of opportunity. For example, short people might well claim that their disadvantage vis-à-vis tall ones in respect to basketball playing could be greatly reduced by ruling that the hoop must be thirty feet from the floor. Should the courts so rule or Congress so decree? That one hesitates over this is due to the feeling that while discrimination would be less, the game might not be as good.

So one can see that the criteria of equality and equality of opportunity are not simple and straightforward. Moreover, they are to a considerable degree inharmonious with one another. In a world where people differ in their natural endowments or their preferences, or both, equality of opportunity will lead to inequality of resulting states (such as income); while if we insist on producing equality of resulting states, we will prevent the working of equality of opportunity.[15]

Need

The idea of need as a criterion of distributive justice is based on the proposition that no member of society should be lacking in what are regarded as the minimum requisites of life. This is the oldest and most continuous principle that has operated in practical terms as a redistributive criterion. In the past it was accepted as a primary obligation of religious institutions, and one Protestant church, the Salvation Army, was founded on the theory that it is not only an obligation but a precondition of religious faith itself. Other social institutions have also played important roles in redistribution on the basis of need. Private altruism has been and continues to be important, but the clear inefficiency of this method, especially in respect to needy persons who have no family or institutional connections, led in late nineteenth-century England to the Charity Organization Society, from which developed modern institutions such as the United Appeal and Community Chest.

One of the main stimuli behind the organized charity movement was the view that providing for the needy by simply dispensing shillings to street beggers from waistcoat pockets might do more harm than good. Part of this reflected the Victorian desire to distinguish between the "deserving" and "undeserving" poor,[16] which tangled the justice idea of "need" up with "desert," but part also reflected the then-growing view that the needy require more than money, and that poverty amelioration should be combined with a program of causal assessment and the prescription of more fundamental remedies. Out of this grew the modern profession of social work. In the twentieth century, all of these obligations have come more and more under the purview of the state, which now operates a vast apparatus aimed at both ameliorating and curing need in a complex variety of ways.

The suggestion has been made that the proper way to define the minimum standard of need is in terms of the income distribution, for example by adopting the rule of considering everyone as needy whose income is less than 50 percent of the society's median income. It is as plausible a need criterion as most others, but it cannot be accommodated without a significant alteration of the general shape of the income distribution; lacking that, there would be the same number of needy persons even if all incomes were increased by ten times or a hundred, or any other finite number. It also pays no attention to the causes of the need: A poor man with faulty kidneys may require command of resources which, if measured as income, would rank him in the high percentiles of the distribution rather than merely bringing him up to half of the median. This is a difficulty that is encountered by all programs that seek to provide for need by some universal mechanical method such as family allowances or the negative income tax.

The half-median rule confuses the idea of need with equality, but it does have the merit of emphasizing the fact that need is a sociological, not a biological, concept. Most of the classical economists recognized this in their efforts to define "subsistence," which played an important role in their theories. Some social welfare systems attempt to measure need or "poverty" on some objective criterion, but these are unavailing and the standard rises steadily as the material welfare of the nonneedy grows. Different societies employ enormously different standards of need, reflecting the general disparity of international incomes.

The vernacular speaks a muffled voice on justice, as on other matters, and anyone who wishes to distinguish between what may be his own philosophical views and those that are commonly held should search for evidence of the latter. Asking people what they believe to be just seems to take direct aim at this question but not necessarily so, for respondents to surveys may say not what they believe but what they think they ought to believe. Observation of what people do rather than what they say provides harder evidence. This evidence seems strongly to suggest that need is the most important criterion of justice in the common judgment. People donate to charity, which remains a flourishing private activity despite the activities of the state, and they respond to disasters to a degree that evidences their willingness to redistribute voluntarily when need is manifest. No organizations exist that collect widely dispersed contributions for the purpose of rewarding desert or merit, or even for decreasing inequality, to the extent that it is separable from need. If we can regard the governmental fisc as reflecting common views, it is significant that little redistribution of income is actually accomplished by taxes; the expenditure side of the state budget does much more, and not by decreasing inequality generally but by raising the low end of the distribution through policies that are clearly need-oriented. Further, one can interpret the ills that people fear most themselves as indicating what resonates on their sense of compassion when observed in others. No one seeks to buy insurance to guarantee that he will get what he deserves or merits, or to assure that his income will not be less than some coefficient of the per capita income; but large sums are spent out of fear of hazards which, should they occur, would make one a member of the needy poor, however deserving.

This is not a claim that the other criteria of justice are absent from the vernacular; only that the principle of need seems to speak with the strongest and clearest voice. This is perhaps no more than a personal-preference ranking of justice criteria as such (some philosophers, e.g. Karl Popper, have expressed a like preference), but I think it reflects something more than that. Need is a very strong theme of welfare, quite independent of justice. It also is an important theme of *freedom* in the views of those who regard freedom positively, as connoting power to do something, and not merely negatively, as absence of coercion by others. So the need criterion of justice receives powerful reinforcement from the two other primary social goods.

Four
Freedom

THE MOST STRIKING characteristic of modern Western political philosophy is the importance in it of personal freedom as a fundamental value. Since the seventeenth century especially this has been a growing theme in both the scholarly and vernacular discussion of social issues, sharply rising at times of upheaval such as during the struggle between the Republic of Venice and the Pope in the early seventeenth century, the English civil war in the mid-seventeenth century, and the American revolutionary war and the French Revolution of the late eighteenth century. In contemporary political thought it continues to be a central issue, not only because Western societies are preteristic, conscious of their *historical* struggle for liberty, but because the success of that struggle remains incomplete and insecure.

The motif of freedom is so strong in the writings of some political philosophers that it overwhelms all other considerations, or at least relegates them to a distinctly lower rank in a lexicographical ordering of values. It may be possible to argue such a priority position for freedom on strictly philosophical grounds or to demonstrate, as John Rawls attempts to do, that any rational, self-interested, risk-averse man would assign it such a superior role, if his judgment could be detached from considerations of personal advantage. In my view, arguments of this sort are not persuasive. Even Rawls finds it necessary to admit that liberty may lose its priority status in societies where the standard of welfare is very low and can be raised by a reduction in personal freedom. The crucial issue is an empirical one: whether in fact the sacrifice of freedom can bring gains in the form of other social goods. If such trades are not empirically possible it is unnecessary to ask whether or under what conditions they are morally permissable. Attention must therefore be directed, in the first instance, to the issue of fact, in order to focus the problem of making choices onto that area where choices are possible.

To tackle this question, we must examine the concept of freedom as a social good, as we have the concepts of welfare and justice in the preceding chapters, since it, like the other two, is not a plain and simple idea. Of the three, it is the hardest to "unpack" in an orderly way and the philosophical difficulties which infuse the concept are compounded, so far as the discourse of vernacular politics is concerned, by the fact that we use the terms "freedom" and "liberty" in an exceedingly wide variety of ways. The English language, normally rich in near-synonyms, in this case requires that two words carry the burden of many meanings.

In ordinary speech we sometimes use the term for descriptive or taxonomic purposes when, for example, we refer to part of the economy as the "free market sector," or we describe the mass media of a country as constituting a "free press." We sometimes divide the whole world into two sectors, one of which is described as the "free world." Value judgments and even ideologies are implied in some such uses of the term, but it would not be correct to say that it always carries ideological connotations. In technical economics, for example, the term "free market sector" is often employed in an almost purely descriptive or taxonomic fashion.

When a travel brochure says that entrance to the Hoosier Forest is "free" there is little ambiguity so far as the tourist is concerned, but the economist is inclined to regard this use of the term as highly misleading, patiently explaining to students and others that it does not mean that the resource costs of operating the facility are zero, but that they are borne by taxpayers rather than by users of the facility.

When a plumber says "the valve is free," he does not mean that it can be acquired without charge, as in making use of the Hoosier Forest; he means that it can operate to perform its function unimpeded by any mechanical constraint. The plumber's usage of the term is similar to the sense in which it is widely employed by political philosophers, indicating the absence of constraints upon action. In human social activity, however, constraints are much more varied than in plumbing. A person may say "I am not free to go to dinner on Friday," and the constraint he has in mind may be that he will be in jail; has another engagement; or expects that food will be served which he is not "free" to eat because of religious allegiance, moral conviction, or medical advice. Or, if the dinner is to be Dutch treat, he may mean that he is not free to go because he lacks money—this indicates a large additional spectrum of constraints, those connected with the production and distribution of income in the economic system. Different constraints again are implied when a teacher says to a student "You are not free to go until you have completed the assignment," or a child says "I *can't* practice the piano now because I am not in the mood for it," or a voter says "I am not free to exercise my political rights because one of the candidates for office is a fool and the other a rogue, and I do not wish to be represented by either." The concept of freedom as absence of constraint will be examined more fully later in this chapter. Even if it could be satisfactorily formulated, however, it would not satisfy a Stoic for whom freedom consists not in the absence of constraints to the satisfaction of one's desires, but the suppression of desire itself. To be free from inner compulsions, however, is clearly not the same thing as to be free from constraints imposed by others.

To complicate matters further, one might note that in common speech the term may be employed to indicate neither the suppression of wants, nor the elimination of constraints to their satisfaction, but to connote a lack of discrimination, as in "She is free with her favors," or "Professor Jones gives A grades freely." We could doubtless go on somewhat further in this way since these illustrations probably have not exhausted the many senses in which the concept of freedom is employed in common speech.

None of the categories of social goods is capable of direct quantitative measurement, but empirical social scientists can justifiably claim that they have achieved some success in devising indexes of the major components of welfare and justice that are of considerable use in the analysis and discussion of public policy. National income accounting has been of great assistance in examination of changes in material welfare and this has been supplemented by a variety of quantitative "social indicators" which are broader in scope. The discussion of justice has similarly been assisted by quantitative measurements of the degree of inequality in income distributions, empirical analysis of the sources of such inequalities, the empirical definition of need, and various other aspects of the issue of justice. These quantitative empirical achievements not only supply some concreteness and precision to the general ideas of welfare and justice, but they have also assisted considerably in the conceptual clarification of these fundamental social objectives.

When we come to freedom, however, we receive little assistance from quantitative empirical research. No one has yet been able to devise any index that can stand as a plausible indicator of the extent of freedom or of changes in it. The most important consequence of this is that, although freedom is widely regarded as a fundamental social good, it does not enter effectively as an element in the determination of public policies. Social scientists estimate the welfare effects of projected policies, or their justice effects in terms of income distribution or other variables, but they would be nonplussed if someone were to ask them to estimate the affects of a policy proposal on freedom. In the modern technical world it is difficult for nonquantifiable values to assert their importance. The doctrinaire libertarian may claim that freedom is infinitely valuable, in confidence that no one can contradict him by presenting a finite measure of it, but it is more likely in the day-to-day examination of public policy, especially within the professional circles where the technical work is done, that what is not measurable is valued at zero. What cannot be counted does not count. Anyone who might be bold enough to ask whether a policy's benefits may not be worth its costs in terms of freedom sacrificed is likely to be regarded, even by economists who are dedicated to comparing benefits with costs, as having thrown a red herring upon the table. Still, one may appreciate the consternation of an empirical social scientist who is asked to consider the freedom costs (or benefits) of a policy, without concluding that such considerations are unimportant, or incapable of rational examination.

Since freedom is here regarded as a primary social good, it is necessary to understand its meaning, conditions, and implications. Ideally one would want to unpack the concept in a way that enables one to arrive at elements that are capable of precise formulation and empirical estimation. Its importance as a social good does not disappear, or even diminish, because we cannot do this, but one should always adapt methods to problems, not the other way round, so the discussion of freedom that follows in this chapter aims at clarifying what, despite all efforts, will remain a highly imprecise concept. Nevertheless, we can be sufficiently concrete so that, in the following chapter, we can examine the vital issue of the ways in which the three primary social goods are in conditions of conflict or congruence with one another.

Freedom and Necessity

A fundamental assumption within the framework of thought that constitutes the scientific attitude is that nothing occurs without cause; no phenomena are autonomous or spontaneous. Since causes are themselves phenomena, they must have causes in their turn, and so on back to the beginning of time. If all phenomena without exception were uniquely determined in this way, including all human phenomena, it would be meaningless to speak of a person as having freedom of action. Even if we were to grant that the human organism has something called "mind," its operations would be as determined by antecedent causes as any other phenomenon. In order to claim that freedom is a meaningful idea and not an illusion (which is also causally determined) it is necessary to assert that human organisms (and perhaps other entities as well) possess some degree of initial autonomy; some power to produce phenomena which act as causal forces but are themselves uncaused in some meaningful sense.

The notion of uncaused causes is not a welcome one to the scientific frame of mind, and the opening it seems to offer to the revival of mysticism is sufficient to make any rationalist exceedingly apprehensive. Isaiah Berlin speaks of "the widespread and influential feeling . . . that science and rationality are in danger if determinism is rejected or even doubted."[1] But the acceptance of determinism is equally unwelcome to the modern rational intellect, and one could also speak of a widespread and influential feeling that much of what is regarded as vital to the human condition is disregarded if determinism is embraced. Some have been led by this apparent dilemma to reject the idea that there can be social "science," arguing that what students of social phenomena do is fundamentally different from the procedures of natural scientists.[2] Historians especially have resisted attempts to inject economic theory or other science-like procedures into their craft. Some, following Ranke, argue that what a historian does is simply to describe events, without any attempt to explain them by asserting causal connections. Others contend that they explain events, but that they do so by procedures which are like those of poets and belles-lettrists, employing intuitive synthetic understanding or *Verstehen*, rather than the procedures by which a scientist arrives at general laws.

The dilemma is, however, a false one. The crux of the issue is whether one may explain social phenomena by reference to such things as individual human "motives" or "beliefs," or "reasons." Can such things be accorded the status of "causes" in general statements about phenomena which are similar to those which natural scientists make? This is a large issue, still under debate among philosophers of science, which we cannot digress to examine here, but it seems to me that it is perfectly sensible, and scientifically valid, to explain material events by pointing to mental factors such as motives or reasons as their causes.[3] If motives and reasons have causal status, one need only assert another sensible porposition, that motives and reasons are not themselves fully determined by material antecedents, in order to claim that there is autonomy, and therefore freedom, in human action, without threatening to destroy the basis of scientific method or its applicability to social phenomena.

Of course, it is still open to anyone to claim that what we call motives or reasons are as determined as the fall of Newton's apple. I see no way of proving to anyone who wishes to make such a statement that he is talking nonsense. Jean-Paul Sartre apparently held the belief that one can defeat a determinist by performing an utterly purposeless act, such as driving a knife through one's hand for no reason. This proves nothing. Moreover, it confuses freedom with caprice, one of the many persisting and pernicious errors of romanticism.[4] It gives no support at all to those who wish to argue, as I do, that freedom should be construed as the ability to engage in purposeful action.

A more important defense of the possibility of autonomous human action has come, in recent years, from within the orbit of natural science itself, through the development of quantum mechanics in physics. This inserts an element of indeterminacy in physical theory, which is regarded by some physicists and philosophers as reflecting an indeterminacy that is a real characteristic of the natural world. The physicist Arthur Compton, for example, embraced the development of quantum mechanics in the early twentieth century not only because of its superiority over Newtonian mechanics as an explanatory model, but because of its philosophical implications for ethics and politics.[5] Sir Karl Popper, one of the leading philosophers of science of our time, has adopted the principle of indeterminacy (in a broader sense) as the foundation of a theory of scientific method, which has won wide support among physical and social scientists,[6] and has elaborated his philosophy of science into a powerful defense of freedom as a fundamental component of political theory.[7] In the social sciences proper the leading figure is Frank Knight who, as a young man, made an important advance in a central area of economic theory by defining the meaning and significance of uncertainty, and spent a large part of the rest of his long scholarly life in further explorations of its philosophical, ethical, and political implications.[8]

Such defenses of philosophical freedom are strong, but not compelling. They do not succeed in proving that indeterminacy is a natural characteristic of the empirical world, so it is still open to the determinist to claim that freedom is an illusion which derives its immediacy from what we do not know rather than from what we do. In one respect however, the determinist is on much weaker ground than the autonomist, since he is bound by the logic of his position to be his own fatal critic. If he insists that men are not free to act otherwise than they do, what is the status of his own action in making such an assertion? All statements, including his own, have no more meaning than the noise of the wind in the trees. If his own statement that the world is deterministic is exempt from this general principle, no demonstration can be offered to prove that it is unique in this respect; other exempt statements can be made, including ones that assert the existence of freedom. The determinist, if he is consistent and correct, must admit that whatever he says is meaningless, and so he dies by his own hand. The autonomist may be wrong, but he is not compelled by the logic of his position to commit suicide, and that seems to be a point in his favor.

The determinism that must be rejected is the radical form of that doctrine, which denies the possibility of any autonomous action whatsoever. But if we are comparing extreme positions, the doctrine of radical autonomy is no better. This would ascribe the existence of something akin to "mind" not only to human and other organisms but also to nonorganic entities such as stones, rivers, and mountains; they too would have motives and reasons that affect their behavior. The natural world would then be replete with spiritual powers and all phenomena could be attributed to their autonomous action. This doctrine, animism, has a much longer history than that of determinism; it still flourishes in primitive societies and, in somewhat more subtle forms, in parts of the most civilized ones as well. One of the appeals which determinism makes to the rational intellect is simply that it is an attack upon animistic superstition. But the extreme forms of both doctrines are rationally unacceptable. Frank Knight once remarked that, having waged a long struggle to escape from the belief that stones are like men, we are now engaged in a struggle against the belief that men are like stones.

Freedom, implying as it does the possibility of autonomous action, is clearly antithetical to radical determinism, but if we do not insist on going to extremes, the relation between freedom and determinism will be seen, on the contrary, to be complementary. The conception of the world as governed by causal laws is, in fact, a precondition of the existence of freedom. Freedom to engage in autonomous acts implies that one can act *purposively*, which is not possible unless the consequences of actions can be predicted with a reasonable degree of reliability. Purposeful action requires two conditions: that the world which one desires to affect is governed by causal laws, and that these laws (or, at least, the regularities which they produce) are known to the actor. Without these two conditions, purposeful action, and therefore freedom, would be impossible.

The second condition, *knowledge* of the (probable) effects of one's action, is as vital to freedom as the existence of causal laws themselves. Aristotle regarded men who are ignorant as like men in chains. As a biological species, man may be no less subject to laws of nature than the herring, but the range of his purposeful action is much larger because he has greater knowledge of the constraints which they impose and can use that knowledge to locate more opportunities for autonomous action. What one is free to do depends upon what one knows. A man may be free to throw a pair of dice in the sense that there are no physical constraints preventing him from engaging in such an act, and he knows about gravity. But he cannot make a free decision to throw a seven on any particular try because, even though the behavior of the dice may be rigidly determined by physical laws, he does not possess the knowledge that is requisite to the performance of a purposeful act of such explicitness.

We may say that his intention was to throw a seven, but we cannot say that the reason why a seven (rather than another number) turned up is because he had this intention. An action may, therefore, be "free" in certain respects and not in others, because the actor is able to predict certain consequences of his action but not others. On July 28, 1914, at Sarajevo, a Serbian nationalist, Ristich, shot and killed the Archduke Ferdinand of Austria. It is meaningful to say that "Ristich freely decided to kill the Archduke" only because one may assume that Ristich had the requisite knowledge of the operation of firearms, ballistics, anatomy and physiology, etc. If Ristich had no more knowledge of these matters than a herring, we could only say something like "At a certain instant on that day, Ristich freely decided to crook the index finger of his right hand." To confine oneself to the latter statement as defining the limits of Ristich's autonomy would be absurd, but it would be equally absurd to say that "Ristich decided to start a war." Ristich possessed no such freedom of action because there are no laws of nature that link assassinations and wars together in a predictable fashion and, even if there are such laws, Ristich did not possess the knowledge of them that is a precondition of purposeful action.

The import of this is that the orbit of freedom is determined by the scope of *reason*. Purposeful action is rational action. In the romantic conception, the free man is one who can exercise his will without constraint. If this were so, the only free men would be those who, like Doctor Faustus, acquire unlimited magical powers, which enable them to disregard even the laws of nature. The rational concept of freedom does not rest upon fancies of this sort. It accepts the existence of immutable natural laws and opens an orbit of freedom by recognizing that there exist points of autonomous action which enable one to *use* the laws of nature, not merely obey them.

The complementarity of causal determinism and freedom, which Franz Neumann significantly calls "the cognitive element in freedom," has a long history, going back to the Greek Epicureans and playing a large role in the philosophies of Spinoza, Hegel, and Marx.[9] As Hegel and Marx demonstrated, however, it is also a dangerous idea which, when extended, leads to a total destruction of freedom. One may begin by asserting that the exercise of freedom requires the "recognition of necessity," then go on to *define* freedom as nothing more than such recognition, and end by declaring that "true" freedom is only attained when one subordinates oneself totally to some "necessity"—the state (in Hegel's case, the Prussian state of his day) or the inevitability of history (as perceived by Marx)—and spends one's time constructing nonsense political slogans such as the desirability of "forcing men to be free."[10] Such extravagances however should not induce one to regard the defense of freedom as requiring rejection of determinism. Any idea can be turned into its opposite by sufficiently skillful casuistry.

The impossibility of exercising freedom in a world that is unpredictable has political implications which have been important, and continue to be important, in real societies. Franz Neumann points out that the belief of the ancient Greeks that natural phenomena are due to the arbitrary interventions of the gods was attacked by Epicurus and Lucretius, and supported by Plato, for reasons that reflect differences of political philosophy more than they do metaphysical preconceptions about the nature of things.[11] Plato sought to promote the ancient superstitions (though it seems that he did not believe them himself) because of their usefulness in keeping the masses in subjection to an elite. In a lawless world, immense power comes into the hands of any who are believed to possess influence, however small, with the gods. It is striking how many ancient and even primitive civilizations achieved the ability to predict eclipses. Why was human ingenuity devoted to acquiring what appears at first sight to be a totally impractical skill? The evidence that this knowledge was kept secret by its possessors, who formed a priesthood of the society, gives us the answer to this question: the ability to predict eclipses was, in fact, of immense practical *political* value to those who possessed it. The blocking out of the sun in midday is a terrifying phenomenon to men who do not know its causes, and the ability of some to predict such events and, seemingly, control them, can be a potent source of political power. Who would dare disobey a priest who has the ability to propitiate or to command the sun? As scientific knowledge of natural phenomena grew and spread, such sources of power were steadily reduced. But this does not mean that terror as a source of support of tyranny is absent in modern societies, nor is it confined to those religions whose doctrine of the afterlife places propitiary powers in the hands of priests. Political terror can be purely secular in form and human in origin. A world of uncertainty can be created by disturbances of the common round of life which reduce the scope of purposeful action by ordinary men. Under such circumstances men may welcome the rise of a dictator who can "make the trains run on time" because, paradoxically, this increases their freedom. Some dictators, such as Lenin, have perceived that their power to control the masses may be increased even by uncertainties that they themselves create, so terror becomes not only a source of tyranny but an instrument for its extension and perpetuation.

The chief political lesson that is to be learned from the rise of science is that knowledge functions as the complement of liberty only when it is widely disseminated. The tribal priests who had learned to predict eclipses appreciated that this knowledge could be a source of power only if it were kept secret. The Pythagoreans recognized the same political potentialities in mathematics, and the Comteans in science generally, including social science. The history of science from, say, the seventeenth century up to the early twentieth has been marked by the wide dissemination of scientific knowledge, but this era is now ended. The complexity of modern science renders its widespread understanding impossible, and a new priesthood of the cognoscenti is rapidly emerging, with increasing political power. Scientific knowledge has been the leading force in the liberation of modern man, by enabling him to manipulate the laws of nature to serve his purposes, and by releasing him from religious superstition. But men may be manipulated too, treated as means to so-called "higher" ends rather than as ends in themselves, and scientific knowledge can be effectively employed for this purpose as well. One of the most difficult and most important of the problems which face modern liberal societies is that of maintaining the service of science to freedom.

Choice, Constraint, and Power

To say that a person is not free to fly because of the law of gravity or to eat three apples when there are only two available directs attention to the constraints imposed upon action by nonhuman factors, which does little to clarify and can do much to confuse the issue of freedom. As T. H. Green pointed out, "every usage of the term [freedom] to express anything but a social and political relation of one man to others involves a metaphor,"[12] and metaphorical speech can be highly misleading. If a person is placed on an island patrolled by gunboats which prevent him from leaving it, his condition would be physically identical to one who was shipwrecked, but it does not contribute to clarity of thought to regard them both as "unfree" in identical senses of that term. Nor does it assist one's understanding of the problem of freedom to direct attention to the extent to which a person is subject to impulses and compulsions which are internal to himself. To say that a person has freed himself from "enslavement" to alcohol or tobacco is not the same thing as saying that he has escaped from a slave labor camp. The emphasis of modern psychoanalysts on the liberation of the psyche, or the effort of the medieval flagellant to conquer sensual desire, are not germane to the problem of freedom. The heart of the problem derives from the fact that man is a social animal, he lives in societies, and the freedom of each is constrained by the actions of others.

Even such a restriction to the orbit of the "social" does not define the range of issues which concern us here with sufficient clarity. Societies are made up of individuals, but culture and custom are features of social life that have real existence and great importance. The range of a person's freedom is restricted by the cultural norms and customary practices of the society in which he lives, both because each individual is molded into a specific culture, and because any idiosyncracies that escape suppression in youth are subject to conformist pressures of various sorts in adulthood. Societies are characterized by very different degrees of cultural constraint. When, for example, an American reads Ruth Benedict's classic analysis of the patterns of Japanese culture,[13] he must be struck by the extent to which personal freedom in that society is restricted by the norms of the culture; restrictions that are imposed on everyone by everyone, and by no one specifically. Within American society it is evident that different degrees of constraint bear upon a Hasidic Jew or a Mormon as compared with a Reform Jew or a Unitarian. This aspect of freedom raises some important issues such as, for example, the ease or difficulty which a person may experience in exercising a desire to engage in nonconformist behavior or to transfer altogether from our culture to another. To examine such questions as aspects of social freedom would, however, divert one into a lengthy discussion that would be peripheral to the main concern of this essay. In what follows, I will restrict myself not only to social freedom, but to that aspect of it that involves the constraints that some men impose on others in a specific fashion—by personal actions, institutional rules, and by the use of the power of the state.

Freedom can be usefully regarded as freedom of choice. This brings into sharp focus the important fact that a constraint upon individual action is a large or a small one depending upon the availability of substitute modes of action. The law that prescribes that one must drive on the right side of the road is not a restriction of personal freedom (or not one worth worrying about) simply because the right and left sides are near-perfect substitutes for one another. Import restrictions and tariffs are not strong constraints if they are not policed effectively, because smuggling is, or has been at times, a close substitute for legal trade. The political vernacular shows an acute appreciation of this point. When the use of cyclamates as a sweetening agent was prohibited in the United States there was hardly any public opposition at all, because saccharin was available, but when the Food and Drug Administration announced in 1977 that it proposed to ban saccharin as well, the protest was immediate and explosive. The weakness of the scientific basis for the ban was not the reason, though it was the overt focal point of the protest, since the cyclamates were banned on no better evidence. In the saccharin case people were faced with a very sharp reduction in their freedom of choice, but not in the cyclamate case.

The definition of freedom in terms of freedom of choice is, however, deficient in one important respect. If the law prohibits the consumption of saccharin, what is the status of the person who does not consume it anyway? Can one say that the law does not restrict his freedom since nothing he wishes to do is constrained by it? However, if the nonconsumer of saccharin were informed by his physician that he had diabetes the prohibition would suddenly become a serious constraint for him. If one takes the view that freedom of choice includes freedom to *change* one's choices, it becomes clear that constraints such as the saccharin prohibition reduce the freedom even of nonconsumers, since they narrow the scope of *potential* choice. Freedom to change one's choices is a very important freedom. If it were not, there would be little argument that could be effectively levied against voluntary slavery or the establishment of a political dictatorship by free elections. Plato pointed out that it is paradoxical to assert that men are free to act but not free to give up their freedom. The conflict here is between freedom of choice and freedom to change one's choices. Anyone who argues that voluntary slavery should be prohibited or that a freely elected dictatorship is illegitimate is, in effect, asserting that freedom to change one's choices takes precedence over freedom of choice itself. The political importance of this in democratic societies containing political parties that are dedicated to the establishment of dictatorship if they achieve power is self-evident.

In the contemporary literature, a great deal of attention has been focused upon the distinction between positive and negative freedom. Some thinkers, such as Isaiah Berlin and Friedrich Hayek, have strongly insisted upon the necessity of defining freedom solely in negative terms as the absence of coercion, but others, equally sincere in their dedication to freedom, have emphasized its positive sense as power to do what one wishes. It is evident from the discussion so far in this chapter that I am unwilling to embrace one of these conceptions to the exclusion of the other. Freedom construed as power to engage in purposeful action is "positive" in nature, and in the first section of this chapter I have attempted to indicate its significance and importance. But freedom as a social concept must recognize the "negative" aspects, which emphasize constraints. It may be true, as Berlin argues, that the positive concept of freedom has been casuistically employed to undermine it.[14] To say to those who are poor that "you have nothing to lose but your chains" may well be merely an invitation to put on a new set. It may also be true that the rich and powerful use the concept of freedom in its negative sense to stifle the efforts of those who are disadvantaged to share their power. But the misuse of the language of

liberty in either of these ways is not a good reason for concluding that one of the conceptions of freedom is valid to the
exclusion of the other.

The debate over positive and negative freedom has been
clarified by MacCallum, who argues that discussion of the
issue, in order to be effective, must focus upon specific freedoms rather than abstract freedom itself.[15] Freedom, Mac-
Callum contends, invariably involves a triadic relationship
that specifies (a) the particular agent whose action is under
consideration; (b) the particular action in question; and (c)
the constraints which may or may not be operative in such a
case. Thus, any statement concerning freedom is of the form:
(a) is free (not free) to do (b) without being limited by (because of) constraint (c). Those who emphasize the negative
concept of freedom focus upon the relation between the
agent and the constraint, while those who emphasize the
positive concept focus upon the relation between the agent
and the action. MacCallum's insistence that all statements
about freedom must be triadic is, however, more useful as
an attack upon the "positive" and "negative" differentiation
than as a general rule that should be followed in all discussions of the problem. The triadic form requires specification,
which is only salutary up to a point. If one is driven by it to
greater and greater degrees of specification, freedom as a
philosophical and political problem would disappear, ob-
scured altogether by the innumerable specific "freedoms" of
the MacCallum triads.

For the purposes of this essay it is necessary to construe
freedom more generally than MacCallum's argument would
allow. Nevertheless, it is useful to dehomogenize it to some
degree in order to examine the question, which will be taken
up in the next chapter, of the extent to which freedom is

congruent with the other primary social goods, welfare and justice. For this purpose we may distinguish three categories of freedom: economic, political, and intellectual.

Economic freedom can be defined primarily in negative terms, as consisting of the absence of constraint in doing what one wishes with one's property. If by "property" is meant anything that has economic value, including not only real and financial assets but personal ones such as labor power, talent, skill, etc., as well, then economic freedom basically means the right to engage in transactions, voluntary on both sides, which transform some forms of property into others, without legal or other constraints.

Political freedom must be defined in more positive terms, as the right to participate in the operation of political processes through which collective decisions are made. It includes the right to stand for office and vote for candidates and to engage in campaigning on behalf of oneself or others. It also includes the right to make representations to holders of political office, and to criticize and discuss their actual and proposed courses of action. The right to propose, and to campaign for, changes in the constitutional order through which the process of collective decision making functions is not excluded from the orbit of political freedom, though the difficult question arises here of the right to engage in promoting constitutional changes that would end political freedom. A purely negative definition of political freedom is inadequate since the effective exercise of one's right to participate in political processes not only requires the absence of constraints, but the provision of facilities of various sorts; for example, public financing of campaigns for office, the availability of mass media, rules or laws that ensure open candidature for office such as party primaries, etc.

Intellectual freedom is the most triadic of the three. It consists of the right to engage in the search for knowledge and the right to disseminate one's findings (and for others to hear of them) without threat of penalties such as imprisonment, loss of livelihood, or public contempt, which would have the effect of closing specific areas of inquiry or preventing their investigation by anyone who is neither foolhardy nor especially courageous. Intellectual freedom, broadly construed, is not confined to expressions of opinion that are arrived at by scientific or even rational processes; it includes also the right to express, and to hear, statements of belief of any kind, including those which the rational person may regard as groundless, mystical, or bizarre.

Some libertarians would object to this differentiation of freedom into economic, political, and intellectual categories (and even more so to efforts such as MacCallum's to focus the debate upon very specific freedoms) on the grounds that freedom is by nature "indivisible." This is an untenable position. If such were the case there would be no freedom at all since there never has existed, and I doubt that there *can* exist, a society of complete freedom. Friedrich Hayek does not go quite so far as to argue the absolute indivisibility of freedom in principle but he claims, as an empirical judgment, that once we commence to give up our liberties we are led down the "road to serfdom," which is a continuous slippery slope with no intermediate stopping place.[16] Some societies may validly be described as tyrannies or serfdoms in the sense that the quantity of personal liberty in them is very small, but history does not show that many (any?) of them arrived at that unhappy state by means of small cumulative steps from a starting point where something like an indivisible absolute freedom was the state of affairs. One would be foolish to deny that at some points in the continuum the road may indeed become very treacherous. Any society that finds itself in such a condition is in danger of losing more of its liberties than its members truly intend to sacrifice, but it is not a continuum that is fraught with such dangers along its entire length. The argument of the extreme libertarian that one must never sacrifice any freedom regardless of what gains may be forthcoming, insofar as it rests upon the empirical proposition that freedom is indivisible, is untenable.

In the following chapter I shall adopt a view that is sharply at variance with the indivisibility thesis: the possibility that different types of freedom may be traded for one another, and that these in turn may be traded for gains in welfare and justice, is regarded as an open question which calls for empirical examination. Before we consider this however, it should be noted that not everyone regards freedom with favor; some important and influential arguments have been made against it.

Arguments Against Freedom

Describing freedom as a primary social good implies that it is good in itself and not merely instrumental to other ends. A large body of modern thinking, including J. S. Mill's great defense of intellectual freedom in his essay *On Liberty*, the orthodox modern economist's defence of economic freedom, and the orthodox modern political philosopher's defence of political freedom, are essentially instrumentalist in that they are efforts to demonstrate what other desirable things will flow from such freedoms. Yet, very few of the defenders of freedom would deny that they regard freedom as good in itself. Some of those who attack freedom may go so far as to deny this, but the main arguments against freedom are efforts to show that it has undesirable implications or consequences, so the defenders and opponents of freedom enter the lists on the same field. The main arguments against freedom may be classified under four broad headings.

(a) *The choice is burdensome.* If freedom is construed as freedom of choice, it appears to follow that the larger the number of possible choices the greater the degree of freedom. But anyone who has had the bewildering experience of having to choose from among seventeen different brands of canned peas in a modern supermarket knows that the unrestricted proliferation of choice opportunities is not necessarily beneficial. Rational choice requires the acquisition of information and comparative analysis, both of which are costly in terms of time, mental energy, and other scarce resources. The optimum degree of variety is less than infinite and may be quite small if information costs and decision-making costs rise rapidly as the number of potential choices increases. One of the arguments for representative democracy as against plebiscitary government is that the costs of choice under the latter system would be excessive if they had to be borne directly by ordinary people as an addition to their normal activities.

Time magazine, in 1954, reported a discussion between Attlee, Vishinsky, and Mikoyan on the meaning of freedom: "At last, through a bewildered interpreter, the three agreed that in the West it meant 'freedom to choose'; in the Communist East it meant 'freedom from having to choose.' "[17] The latter view, despite its form as a definition of freedom, is really a rejection of freedom, but it cannot be dismissed out of hand as simple casuistry. If people were *forced* to choose carefully among seventeen different brands of peas, a large number of candidates for Congress, and so on, one might well conclude that the architect of such a system had invented a new and ingenious form of tyranny. But if people are not forced to expend their time and energy in this way; if what is open to them is the *opportunity* to make such choices, and to devote as much effort to them as they wish; then there is no undesired burden of choice which people cannot avoid by their own individual efforts. This attack on freedom therefore fails to carry, despite the fact that it has to be admitted that making choices is indeed burdensome.

(b) *That responsibility is burdensome.* The classic exposition of this argument against freedom is Ivan's fable of the Grand Inquisitor in Dostoyevsky's *The Brothers Karamazov*. Whenever a man is able to choose among alternative courses of actions he cannot avoid bearing moral responsibility for the consequences of what he does. The argument of the Grand Inquisitor is that this burden is so heavy that, for ordinary men, it greatly outweighs the benefits of freedom. The Church, says the Inquisitor, has labored for centuries to improve man's lot by relieving him of freedom and taking the weight of responsibility upon itself.

One cannot deny that responsibility is burdensome; common empirical experience indicates that most men seek to limit the responsibility they have to bear, and some are evidently willing to contract the scope of their freedom to quite narrow limits if they can thereby escape the responsibility that accompanies the power of choice. However, the weakness of the Inquisitor's argument can be perceived if we shift it from its theological context to a political one. When men give up their freedom to a dictator, does this mean that responsibility is transferred from them to him? If there were a just God, the moral account might be presented in the other world, but in this world it need not be, and it is less likely to be, the greater the power of the dictator. The political meaning of dictatorship is that the empirical connection between power and responsibility is broken. The dictator is not accountable for his actions and, by contrast, his subjects may be made accountable, and heavily so, by whatever standards he chooses to impose.

Freedom is an impure good since it involves the burdens of choice and responsibility, and the optimum amount of it is unlikely to be the same for all. To the extent that a person retains the most vital of all freedoms, the freedom to *change* his choices, he may experiment with different ways of life and suit his own tastes as to how much responsibility he wishes to bear. Political freedom defined as the *opportunity* to participate in the process of collective choice has some of the characteristics of a "public good," which makes it difficult to supply different amounts of it to different persons but, more importantly, since it deals with the exercise of sovereign power, it is not possible to give up freedom of political choice without losing the power to change one's choices. The Grand Inquisitor did not hold an office that was periodically open to popular election.

(c) *That wisdom is not widespread.* Adam Smith's defense of freedom was grounded upon the proposition that each man is the best judge of his own interests. Many others have argued the reverse, and pointing out that people often make unwise choices, have grounded their social philosophies on the need for control of men's actions by those of them who *are* wise. This is not the same as the argument that it is undesirable, for some reason, to minister to men's individual interests; it accepts the merit of doing so, but contends that many (most?) people are incapable of perceiving what their "real" or "true" or "long-run" interests are. The description of this argument as "paternalistic" is indicative of its nature. Humans are altricial animals requiring a lengthy period of both biological and social development before maturity is attained. It is unavoidable that children must be coerced, since they clearly lack the information and judgment that is necessary to the making of decisions which are wise. Nature assures that almost all human organisms become biologically nature at about the same age but there is no reason to believe that all become competent judges of their own interests when they attain a certain age; everyone knows numerous instances of palpable incompetence that lasts indefinitely. If one regards this as characteristic not of special cases, but of the generality of men, it becomes an argument against freedom in the broad sense.

In opposing this argument it is not necessary to cling to Adam Smith's proposition that every man is the best judge of his own interests or even to contend that this is true of most men. It is sufficient to recognize the difficulty of selecting those who would do better. Nature provides parents for children automatically, and does not invariably make a good job of it. Political processes may be more discriminating than procreational ones but there is little warrant for believing that even the best of them can act as an effective selector of governors whose wisdom and benevolence are so great and so reliable that the rest of mankind should place themselves under their paternal control. Adam Smith also pointed out that some activities are not likely to be worse performed than by those who have the audacity to believe that they are the ones who should be entrusted with them.

Any political system whose main task is to select a "father of the people" is likely instead to select a slavemaster.

(d) *That freedom conflicts with other social goods.* Some ethical philosophers have argued that the nature of things is such that all good things are harmonious. If that were so there would be no problem of choice at all since this always involves sacrificing some goods in order to obtain others. Some defenders of freedom argue that *freedom* at least has the special characteristic that it cannot be exchanged for anything else that is good.[18] As a general proposition this is difficult to defend since innumerable cases can be cited in which such a trade is clearly possible. The discipline known as "welfare economics" consists largely of the analysis of such cases. The extensive, and growing, restriction of economic freedom in modern democratic societies is based mainly on the argument that such freedom conflicts with the attainment of other social goods.

This is the most important argument against freedom. It cannot, however, be advanced in general terms as an unspecified argument against "freedom" as such. Some freedoms may be in conflict with some other social goods, but other relationships may be characterized by congruence. The issue is an empirical one, not one of principle. The next chapter is an attempt to examine these empirical relationships to some degree.

Five
Complementarity and Conflict among Social Goods

OVER THE PAST CENTURY, the branch of social science now called microeconomic theory has been developed into a highly sophisticated analysis of the problem of how rational choices may be made among alternative courses of action. The theory has proved to be a powerful instrument of practical application, enabling economists to offer more penetrating explanations of economic phenomena and more reliable prescriptions for social policy. In the last decade or so, the methods of microeconomic theory have been extended to a wider range of subjects, hitherto regarded as belonging to the other social sciences: sociology, political science, history, etc. The recent works of Rawls, Nozick, and Buchanan, frequently referred to in these pages, represent attempts to apply microeconomic theory even to the most fundamental problems of political philosophy, the derivation of ethical principles which should govern the exercise of the sovereign power of the state. In the light of these developments, it would seem that the next step that should be taken in this

book is to apply the logic of rational choice which economists have constructed to the problems delineated in the
preceding chapters. Having classified all goods under three
headings—welfare, justice, and freedom—should one now
proceed to develop theorems that define the optimum mixture of them? In this chapter I wish to take up the vital issue
of choosing among primary social goods, but I will not do so
by rigorously employing the analytical model of microeconomic theory, because only a *part* of that model is applicable
to this problem. The part that *is* applicable can be used to
clarify the problem of social choice and, I hope, enable us to
make better choices, but it cannot generate definitive or precise theoretical solutions.

In order to operate the choice logic of microeconomic
theory one must have two types of information: (a) information concerning the objective world's "transformation structure," which tells us how much of one good may be obtained
by sacrificing some quantity of another good; and (b) information about the chooser's subjective "preference structure," which tells us how much of one good would have to be
obtained in order to compensate him for a loss of some
quantity of another good. We cannot apply the procedures of
microeconomic theory to the problem of determining the optimum mixture of welfare, justice, and freedom because the
second of these two information requirements is unob-
tainable. In dealing with concrete consumer goods, economic theory assumes that, despite the great variety of them
and the different wants they satisfy, they are commensu-
rable with one another simply because they do satisfy wants.
They are useful, in this sense of that term; that is, they provide utility. This common factor is construed to be what the
consumer maximizes and the problem of rational choice

then becomes a matter of delineating the conditions of utility maximization.

As I have already indicated, the utilitarian calculus is not without difficulties when applied to concrete consumer goods. Nevertheless, economic theory based upon this calculus has proved to be exceedingly valuable as an explanatory model of empirical economic phenomena and as a prescriptive procedure for a large range of practical problems. Its capabilities are not unlimited, however. The choice logic of microeconomic theory cannot be employed to determine the optimum mixture of welfare, justice, and freedom because these goods do not share a common quality which can function as the choice maximand at the level where choices among them must be made. As a result, we cannot construct the necessary preference structure. Such a preference structure can be developed for the components of welfare alone, by construing it in individualistic terms and regarding the social welfare as the additive sum of individual welfares. This distorts the human condition, but not so grossly that the analysis is invalidated. Justice and freedom, however, are fundamentally *social* in nature. For a single individual, such goods could be included in his own utility function or preference structure but one could not aggregate the individuals by any known (or conceivable?) procedure without destroying the problem instead of solving it. This is the reason why economists have had so little success in attempting to incorporate justice issues, such as the distribution of income, into their prescriptive models, and why issues of freedom remain securely entrenched within the disciplines of political and moral philosophy, immune from the powerful colonizing propensities of modern economics. Welfare, justice, and freedom are incommensurable social goods in the sense that it is not possible to construct a *social* preference structure composed of them that is analogous to the preference structure for consumer goods which is a vital element in the choice logic of economic theory. This lacking, we must tackle the problem of how to determine the desirable mixture of such social goods in a different way.

One such way (which, in my view, quickly runs into a blind alley) is to attempt to construct a "lexicographical" ordering of social goods. The want that is served by the first good in this order must be "fully" satisfied (whatever that may mean) before one goes on to serve the second want; the second before the third; and so on. This argument goes further than I would in denying the preference substitutability of goods. It contends not only that they are not substitutable in the way that is necessary to operate the choice logic of microeconomic theory, but that they are not substitutable at all. One writer has adopted the extreme position that, even in personal preferences, goods are lexicographically arranged, starting with those that satisfy physiological requirements, then going on to safety, love, and self-actualization, in descending order.[1] It is unwise to quarrel with anyone else's preferences for things that serve his personal wants, but I think that this scheme is, to say the least, idiosyncratic. As a statement of what is typical it is falsified by even the most casual empirical observation. But arguments of this sort do not concern us here, except as extreme examples of the lexicographical ordering approach, since they are not germane to the issue of social policy. Much more important is John Rawls's contention that liberty and distributive justice are arranged in such an order.[2] This is advanced as an ethical proposition, that is to say, as a rule that social policy must follow if it is to be morally sound.

Lexicographical ordering appears to simplify the problem of making choices among social goods, just as the conventional alphabetic order simplifies the task of the dictionary maker. It does not, however, provide us with a method for making choices; it tells us instead that there is one and only one mixture of social goods that is ethically proper: that which sacrifices no higher-order good to any lower-order good regardless of how much or how little of each the society has. This really eliminates the problem of making choices rather than furnishing a method for dealing with it. When faced with the necessity of choosing among social goods, the decision maker is not in an analogous position to that of the consumer allocating a budget, but his problem is not analogous to that of the dictionary maker either, and it cannot be made so by ethical theorizing.

Lexicographers need not engage in dispute as to what is the proper ordering for the letters of the alphabet since any order that is generally understood will serve; nor need they entertain much doubt as to what is meant by the letters *A*, *B*, etc., or what specific written letters come under each generic classification, *A*, *B*, etc. But rational persons may entertain quite different views concerning the meaning and content of terms like "freedom," "justice," and welfare"; and even if this were as clear as the alphabet, there would be a great deal of difference of opinion as to what the proper order should be since this is not a mere matter of convenience but a vital issue in ethical and political philosophy. Rawls fails to demonstrate that his procedure generates a lexicographical ordering of social goods that is sufficiently compelling to end dispute on this point and I do not think that an ordering of this sort is demonstrable by any analytical procedure. Moreover, the idea of such an ordering implies that the value of additional amounts of a social good is independent of the quantity of it one already has. This is not an acceptable view of the nature of rational preference structures. One does not have to reduce social goods to "utility" in order to recognize that something akin to the law of diminishing marginal utility applies to them in the preferences of rational persons.

I do not mean to imply that the social goods classified as welfare, justice, and freedom are totally independent of one another. We do trade them for one another, we must, and we should. Choosing among them is both practically necessary and, it seems to me, morally permissible. What I am arguing is that such choosing cannot be done by following the procedures of economic theory since these goods cannot be reduced, in the social preference structure, to something intelligible that can play the role of maximand. In short, this is not a scientifically soluble problem. Determining the optimal mixture of welfare, justice, and freedom is, indeed, the most fundamental task of politics.

The other side of the choice logic of economic theory, however, the "transformation structure," is as germane to the mechanism by which choices are made by means of politics as it is to the technical procedures of economic theory. No method of choice can be satisfactory (one is tempted to say "rational") if it neglects the relevant facts of the real world. So it is desirable that we know as much as we can about the empirical trading possibilities among social goods.

It has sometimes been argued that this problem of choice is constrained by the fact that one special social good is, empirically, a precondition of all others. This, in effect, elevates it to priority status, not as a matter of preference or ethical judgment, but as a matter of fact. The doctrine of Ludwig von Mises and Murray Rothbard, for example, claims such status for private property rights and economic freedom. In a more metaphysical vein, others have argued, following Leibnitz, that there *cannot* be any empirical conflict between social goods since the world generally is a harmonious system or, following Spinoza, that there is harmony at least among those things that are good. If the precondition argument or the Spinozan harmony argument were correct, the problems of politics would be much simplified; if the Leibnitzian harmony argument were correct there would be no need for politics at all. Empirical propositions are empirical, however; they cannot be sustained by metaphysical or doctrinal propositions, so our task is to examine this issue in an empirical way, without predetermining the results by a priori declarations. In this chapter I shall attempt to make some progress in this direction. It will be small, but I hope that it may serve to open a line of investigation that will prove fruitful.

The main difficulty that attends any attempt to examine the transformational relationships between social goods is that the number of these potential relationships is very large, much larger than the number of goods themselves. This is due to the fact that, unlike the transformation functions used in the economic theory of production, the relationship between any pair of social goods is not one relationship but two, since each of the goods may be an independent variable, or "cause" as I shall call it, and each may be a dependent variable, or "consequent." Thus, in considering the transformational relations between welfare and justice, for example, we have to consider separately the effect that a change in the level of welfare may have upon justice and the effect that a change in justice may have upon welfare, since the latter is not merely the inverse of the former. Consequently, if we consider only *three* social goods, welfare, justice, and freedom, we have to examine *six* cause-consequent relationships:

> The effect of a change in welfare on justice
> The effect of a change in welfare on freedom
> The effect of a change in justice on welfare
> The effect of a change in justice on freedom
> The effect of a change in freedom on welfare
> The effect of a change in freedom on justice

If we call the number of cause-consequent relationships R and the number of primary goods N, then

$$R = N^2 - N$$

and it is plain that R increases very rapidly as N is increased. If we were to attempt to work with, say, 100 goods, we would have to examine 9,900 cause-consequent relationships; and if we added one more good, the number of relationships would increase to 10,100.

This exponential multiplication of relationships is the reason why the ordinary discussion of social issues, even among rational and openminded persons, is often ineffectual; the attempt to consider all aspects of any issue leads one into a jungle of complexity. It is hardly surprising therefore that social philosophers and social scientists have attempted to simplify the problem. Lexicographical ordering is one form of simplification, which operates by regarding goods as independent of one another without limit. The choice logic of economic theory is another method which, by reducing all goods to "utility," that is, a common numeraire, makes $R = N$, thus avoiding at least the exponential multiplication of relationships. It is obvious, however, that if one eschews any and all simplifying procedures the problem becomes unmanageable. In the foregoing chapters I have found it necessary to distinguish ten social goods—two types of welfare: material and cultural; five criteria of justice: fair exchange, desert, equality, equality of opportunity, and need; and three categories of freedom: economic, intellectual, and political. Even if these were homogeneous goods (which I have been at pains to deny) we would have to examine ninety cause-consequent relationships, which is unworkable. Restricting the entities to what I have employed as classificatory categories, i.e., welfare, justice, and freedom, reduces the number of relationships to six, but this proves to be unworkable for other reasons. The minimum number of goods with which I have found it possible to operate is five: welfare, justice, and the three categories of freedom. This requires the examination of twenty cause-consequent relationships. In the remainder of this chapter I will endeavor to undertake such an examination as systematically as I can, consolidating the findings at the end.

Before embarking on this, it is essential to note that in what follows I will be focusing upon the empirical cause-consequent relationships between pairs of social goods in terms of *incremental* changes in the causes, and with reference to the state of affairs which seems to pertain in contemporary Western democracies, most particularly the United States. The disposition of some political philosophers to delineate the importance, say, of economic freedom by examining the extreme point at which it is zero is not useful. This is, in essence, a version of Adam Smith's water-diamonds paradox, by which he concluded that the usefulness of a commodity could have nothing to do with explaining its market price since water is essential to life while diamonds serve much less important wants. Smith's empirical observation was true but irrelevant to the value problem, for the problem of choice, in orderly societies at least, is always a matter of exchanging marginal quantities. It is easy to show, for example, that if there were no economic freedom at all—if a central authority determined everyone's employment, his ability to obtain paper and other means of expression of opinion, his access to books, radio programs, etc.,—then there would be little or no intellectual freedom either, or political freedom; and there would probably be low standards of welfare and justice as well. This is not an irrelevant point to make concerning some societies, but it does not prove that in the contemporary Western democracies *full* economic freedom (whatever that might mean) is a precondition of everything else that is good. The region of a transformation function that is relevant is that which is contiguous to where one is. In the following attempt to examine the relationships between the three categories of freedom, and between them and the other social goods, I will confine myself to that region that seems to be inhabited by contemporary democracies.

Before going any further, I should note, in order to avoid misunderstanding, that I am not happy with the terminology employed in the following analysis. "Causal" and "consequential" are excessively strong terms, having connotations of direct causality which I do not always intend to imply. "Independent variable" and "dependent variable" would not be any better. The reader should keep in mind that I am speaking only of the empirical transformational *relationships* between goods, without necessarily implying that they are always due to a causal connection in the strict sense.

Economic Freedom as Causal Variable

Intellectual Freedom as Consequent [−]

The minus sign which is noted as pertaining to this relationship indicates that, in some respect that is not of negligible significance, there is a conflict between economic freedom and intellectual freedom; that is to say, the exercise of economic freedom in some way reduces intellectual freedom in some way or, conversely, certain restrictions of economic freedom result in gains to intellectual freedom. When the relationship between two goods is complementary in some important respect, increases (decreases) in the causal variable resulting in increases (decreases) in the consequential one, a plus sign will be employed.

Economic freedom, defined as the ability to do what one wishes with one's property, appears to be a pure good if one adds the condition that all exchanges of property between contracting parties are voluntary. It is true that no party to a voluntary exchange can be harmed by it, assuming that everyone is fully informed. But, as welfare economists have long recognized, the legal system does not require that everyone who is affected by a transaction (or other uses of property) must be a recognized party. Transactions take place, not between all affected parties, but only between those who have established legal claims. The existence of "external" effects, that is, effects on those who are not parties to the exchange, means that even voluntary exchange cannot be regarded with unqualified approval. This raises the issue of potential conflict between economic freedom and welfare, which looms large in the modern theory of welfare economics. We will have to take note of this later; at this point, I wish to show that an analogous problem arises in respect to the relationship between economic freedom on the one hand and intellectual freedom on the other.

In purely theoretical terms, it is possible to conceive of a market system in which all those affected by a transaction or other use of private property must give their voluntary consent. Thus, for example, it is not theoretically inconceivable that a steel mill should obtain the consent of those affected by its smoke, presumably by compensating them for their inconvenience. The practical difficulties of doing so are very great and all but the most doctrinaire devotees of free markets recognize that it is necessary to constrain actions that produce air pollution by some form of collective action, by the state or some other agency that has statelike powers, since those who are affected by the pollution are both numerous and dispersed and it is not practically possible for each to negotiate on his own account. The effect of private actions that exercise freedom to use one's property as one wishes can have similar effects upon the intellectual freedom of others that are not of negligible importance. If a city is served by two newspapers, a voluntary agreement of sale between their owners which eliminates one of them as an independent editorial entity reduces the access of the citizenry to alternative sources of information and commentary. If the general public had to be compensated for this loss, the sale might not take place. Obviously, it is even less feasible to require that this be done than to require that those affected by smoke pollution be compensated, the losses involved being less tangible, less calculable, and more individual in their nature.

In a society that has numerous media of mass communication—newspapers, magazines, books, the electronic media, etc.—the sale of one newspaper to another may not be of great significance. But anyone who regards intellectual freedom as dependent upon access to a variety of sources, as both a consumer of media content and as a potential contributor to it, cannot view with equanimity the development of newspaper chains, the creation of electronic media networks, and the common ownership of different types of media. The right to do what one wishes with one's property, when the property in question has to do with serving the demand for information and opinion, is an economic freedom that is subject to constraints which are at least as justifiable by empirical evidence as those which are imposed on those who generate more tangible externalities such as air pollution. This argument, it should be noted, does not apply only to media that are privately owned in the usual sense. Ownership by trustees, foundations, labor unions, political parties, religious institutions, and governments does not obviate the problem, since it results not from the profit orientation of private enterprise, but from concentration of editorial power and the reduction of variety. At the present time, there is a large degree of variety in the mass media and other sources of information and opinion in the United States and other democratic countries, but it would be foolish, in my view at least, to regard the growth of concentration in this area as unimportant. As an empirical matter then, the relationship between economic freedom and intellectual freedom cannot be regarded as one of full congruence. To do what one wishes with one's property may conflict with intellectual freedom when the property in question provides intellectual services.

I should emphasize at this point that, in placing a minus sign on the relationship between economic freedom and intellectual freedom at the head of this section, I do not mean to imply that there is a *general* conflict between them. The notation indicates only that there is a conflict in the *specific* respect that is indicated in the subsequent discussion. The same restriction applies also to the notations applied to the following section headings.

Political Freedom as Consequent [+ and −]
In certain important ways the exercise of economic freedom contributes to political freedom and the two are complementary, but there are also some conflicts between them, as indicated by the above notation. I will discuss their complementarity first. A regime of political freedom cannot be construed as resulting from voting procedures alone. Even if all public policies were determined by plebiscites, a necessary component of such a regime is public debate. This activity is not costless, for the capacity to engage in debate is not unlimited. Resources that are used for one purpose are not available for others, time and mental energy being scarce goods. The market mechanism acts as a complement to political freedom because it enables the society to make more efficient use of its political resources, by relieving the political system of the burden of performing tasks that can be handled as effectively, or more so, in other ways.

The economic processes of a society could be organized through the political system. The provision of "public goods" must be organized in this way for reasons that are well known. This could be extended to goods that are not "public" ones for technical reasons, but every such extension uses up some of the political system's capacity to make decisions. If an economy were completely planned and directed by a central authority, the political system would be responsible for determining the allocation of productive resources in specific terms. Detailed directions concerning the quantities and qualities of goods and services to be produced, and the methods to be used to produce them, would have to be issued by central authority. This is a formidable task, even in the computer age. If it were attempted by a society in which political decisions are made, not dictatorially, but by open and widespread political participation, the mechanism of politics would break down from sheer overburden. There is, of course, another way to organize economic processes so as to allocate scarce productive resources: by means of a market mechanism in which people exercise freedom to engage in voluntary exchange. To the extent that private markets perform this function, the political system's decision-making capacity can be devoted to other things. There are many decisions that *cannot* be made through the automatic mechanism of markets and it may be that, in modern society, the capacity of politics to cope effectively is severely taxed by them alone, but it would clearly be overburdened if it were called upon not only to manage foreign policy, national defense, the control of crime, the provision of public goods, support for the needy, etc., but also to determine what types and styles of shoes, automobiles, foods, etc., to produce and how to produce them. One of the essential roles of private market exchange is simply to release the political system from responsibility for tasks that can be done efficiently by the former, so that the latter is better able to do those things which it, and it alone, must do.

It may seem that I am arguing here from an extreme case which is not relevant to contemporary society. No modern economy, even those of the most centralized dictatorships, operates without markets. Just as a democratic society would break down from overburden if all economic processes were managed by the political sector, so too would a dictatorship. But breakdowns are rare in either type of political system, so what empirical evidence do we have that a democratic political system's capacity for decision making is overloaded? Is economic freedom complementary to political freedom under conditions that are currently relevant in societies like that of the United States?

It is tempting to infer that a political system is overloaded when it is unable to provide solutions for social problems. This is not a valid criterion of judgment if we are looking for "solutions" that are akin to those that engineers and other technicians are able to provide for their kinds of problems. The task of politics, as I argued in chapter 1, is to "cope" with problems that do not have such technical solutions. So the fact that the political system must deal over and over again with the same problem is not evidence that the system does its job badly. Even if policies are less effective than they might be according to "coping" criteria, or even if they are demonstrably incorrect or perverse, one cannot validly infer that this is due to overburden, since there are numerous other factors that affect the ability of any political system to perform effectively.

A prima facie case can, however, be made that the political system is overburdened, in a way that is inimical to political freedom, when powers of decision making are transferred from persons who are accountable for their acts to those who are not. In a political democracy this insulation from responsibility takes place when the professional bureaucrat is able to exercise discretionary powers not subject to the rule of law and, a fortiori, when he acquires the ability not only to execute public policy but to *make* policy. The trend in this direction is one of the most important developments in the political systems of modern democratic states. It will be examined more fully in the next chapter where the issue of the control of coercive power is discussed. That it represents a serious erosion of political freedom has frequently been noted by observers of the contemporary political scene. The question that is relevant here, however, is why does such growth in bureaucratic power occur? It cannot be due to the fact that politicians are unwilling to exercise power themselves. People who enter the political arena as candidates for public office presumably have a desire to exercise power. Why do they allow it to slip from their hands after they are elected to the seat of sovereignty? The answer, in my opinion, is that they are overburdened. This may be due to the tendency of the modern state to do too much in some aggregate sense, but it could also be due to the assumption by the state of tasks that make especially heavy demands upon the limited capacity of the decision-making system. When the state undertakes to regulate prices and other terms of exchange, for example, it assumes a formidable responsibility which it invariably discharges by placing coercive powers in the hands of bureaucrats. To the extent that such tasks can be performed by the mechanisms of markets the burden on the political system is reduced without the adoption of methods that threaten the preservation of political freedom. One need not be a doctrinaire conservative in order to claim that the modern state undertakes tasks that would be better left to the private market sector; all that is necessary is the recognition of the relevance of the principle of comparative advantage to the allocation of responsibilities. For some tasks, the administrative burden is so heavy that it is not a question of whether they shall be performed by markets or by politics, since the only practical alternative to the market is the bureaucratic, not the political, system. Even if the bureaucracy were to perform somewhat more efficiently than the market, an argument can still be made against the devolution of political powers to it on grounds of preservation of political freedom.

This does not mean that freedom to engage in market exchange or otherwise to use one's property as one wishes is complementary to political freedom without limit. Freedom to buy and sell shoes or vegetables or labor services under competitive conditions is one thing; freedom to use one's economic resources to buy votes or to bribe politicians, judges, or officials is another matter. In all democratic states such uses of property are proscribed, some with severe penalties. In recent years these restrictions have been extended to the use of personal or institutional property in support of candidates for political office or to lobby for or against specific pieces of legislation. Public policies of this sort are based on a recognition that in some respects, economic freedom and political freedom are in conflict.

If one were prepared to say that a public policy is justified by having widespread popular support, we could simply note that such restrictions on economic freedom apparently enjoy such support, but even one who thinks that public opinion in a society of intellectual freedom should be given great weight is on weak ground if he is content to rest the matter there. A freely formed public opinion can sometimes be wrong, so we must ask, in a more penetrating fashion, why it seems desirable to restrict the freedom to use economic resources in order to buy votes, bribe legislators, etc. If a person is willing to spend X dollars in support of a legislative proposal does that not mean that its passage is more valuable to him than its defeat is to another person who is willing to spend less than X dollars for that result? If we are prepared to say that competitive markets allocate goods and productive resources efficiently when they go to the highest bidder, why should it not do likewise for votes?

Asking questions of this sort reveals the crux of the issue. The political system of a democratic state is based on the principle of "one man, one vote," whereas the market system's principle is "one dollar, one vote." Of course, no political system effectively distributes power equally; the object of rationing votes according to persons, and prohibiting black markets which would reallocate them according to dollars, is simply an effort to achieve a distribution of political influence that is *more* equal than the distribution of economic wealth or income.[3] In dictatorships the distribution of political power is invariably more concentrated than the distribution of economic power. The argument that the reverse is an essential condition of a regime of political freedom rests on the fact that the political system is the repository of sovereign power. It not only provides public services such as roads and defense and sewers; it establishes the general framework of rules that govern the actions of people in their private activities. To anyone but a philosophical anarchist it is plain that competitive market activity must be bounded by constraints. (Bombing the factory of a rival enterprise, for example, is not the kind of competitive activity which economic theory regards as contributing to an efficient allocation of resources.) If the ration coupons of political power were for sale, we would live in a plutocracy, not a democracy; the framework of rules would be determined by those who have economic power and they would be designed by them to prevent change in the distribution of power, including such changes as might come about from economic innovation. Political freedom, construed as wide opportunity for participation in the sovereign process of lawmaking, is necessary to orderly change. If political power were for sale, it would certainly produce changes in our present society, but only until it became a full plutocracy, after which all change would cease and a new feudal age would be established wherein economic and political powers were conjoined and ossified. A dictatorial society might be greatly improved by auctioning off coupons of political power to those prepared to pay for them, but not a democratic one. The vernacular intuition that votes should not be salable and, more generally, that the use of economic resources to influence the political process should be restricted, has a sound basis.

One should note that the argument made here is not limited to the use of economic power by wealthy individuals or business corporations. It applies also to that which may be exercised by labor unions, pension funds, foundations, religious institutions, and even public interest associations. Whenever economic power is concentrated it threatens political freedom. The threat is less when there is more than one such center of concentration with opposing aims, but even so, it is necessary to restrict their economic freedom to use the resources at their disposal to buy political influence in a direct fashion. When this way of influencing the political process is constrained, those who wish to exert such influence must divert their efforts to the area of public debate. The ability to affect public opinion is not unconnected with the power to command economic resources, but these are not proportional to one another by any means, so the distribution of political power does not correspond to that of economic power, thus providing opportunities for the exercise of the former by persons who have relatively little of the latter.

Justice as Consequent [+ and −]

Economic freedom is complementary to justice in some respects and in conflict with it in others. This is due to the fact that justice is not a simple good but, as argued in chapter 3, consists of a variety of principles and criteria which cannot be resolved into a harmonious compound. If one accepts the "desert" criterion of justice, where a person's desert is construed to spring from the contributions he makes to the society's production of goods and services, it is clear that economic freedom plays an important role in promoting justice to the extent that the mechanism of voluntary exchange provides a proper valuation of those contributions and transmits such valuations from the product markets back to the factor markets where incomes are determined by wage rates and other factor prices. A centrally directed economy could undertake to reward people according to their contributions, but it too would have to use the market process, or some analogous device, in order to evaluate contributions and to link them effectively with rewards.

But desert is only one criterion of justice for which good arguments can be made. If "need" is accepted as a valid criterion, then it is apparent that one must either rely exclusively on private benevolence to accomplish redistributions of income by voluntary action, or the freedom to dispose of one's economic resources as one wishes must be restricted. The use of coercive power to provide for the needs of unfortunates is a characteristic of all but the most primitive societies and, though it has never been free of great problems, it reflects a nearly ubiquitous perception, valid in my view, that voluntary action is insufficient. The same point can be made with respect to "equality" and "equality of opportunity" as justice criteria. Serving them effectively requires certain limitations of economic freedom.

Even if one were prepared to adopt the view that the only valid criterion of justice is "commutative justice"—that justice consists of what results from a process of fair voluntary exchange—the economic freedom-justice relationship would not be unambiguously complementary. Commutative justice clearly requires economic freedom, but this cannot be extended to actions that produce monopolization of markets, actions that generate dispersed external costs, or actions that are fraudulent or depend upon the ignorance of other parties, so, even based on the principal of commutative justice, there is a wide range of cases that calls for restrictions on freedom to use one's economic resources as one wishes.

Welfare as Consequent [+ and −]

The relationship between economic freedom and welfare is one of the main subjects of modern economic theory. If the system of production is to work efficiently to meet the wants of consumers then it is necessary that adequate information concerning these wants be transmitted to those who make production decisions. Even if the production system were socialized, allocative efficiency would still require an effective signaling mechanism to perform this task, and most socialist economists now recognize the value of markets as part of such a mechanism. In a private enterprise economy, factors of production are also exchanged in markets and the efforts of entrepreneurs to maximize profits translate consumer preferences into production decisions. For these reasons, the effect of economic freedom on welfare is complementary. But it is not unambiguously so, for the following reasons.

Markets do not produce allocative efficiency when monopoly elements are present, so it is necessary to constrain private efforts to exert such market power, and to control the actions of production entities that cannot operate efficiently without encompassing a large share of the total supply. In addition there are various types of market failure, due to the existence of externalities and the like, which have been extensively analyzed since Sidgwick and Pigou brought the issue to the notice of economists by their work on what has become known as "welfare economics." Considerations of this sort require that, in the interest of allocative efficiency, the operations of economic freedom must be constrained in certain respects. Also, there is recognition of the need for state action to protect people from hazards which are not adequately covered by private exchange, such as unemployment, accident, ill health, and inadequate provision for old age. Education also has long been recognized as inoptimally provided if left solely to transactions between private parties. For these various reasons the connection between economic freedom and welfare is conflictual as well as complementary.

These arguments concerning the effect of economic freedom on welfare are parallel to those made above with respect to the effect of economic freedom on justice. The repetition of them is not redundant because in order to maintain as much clarity as we can in these matters, welfare and justice must be construed as different primary goods. The parallelism of the arguments on these two points reveals that restriction of economic freedom on grounds such as one finds in modern microeconomic theory derives support from both welfare and justice considerations, which makes such arguments all the more important. It deserves emphasizing, though, that one cannot make any general argument for the restriction of economic freedom such as that which is advanced by socialist ideologues. Economic freedom is conflictual to welfare and justice in certain respects, but complementary to it in others, so the policies which are required must be developed from consideration of specific cases.

Intellectual Freedom as Causal Variable

Economic Freedom as Consequent [+]

In the preceding section we considered the effect of economic freedom upon intellectual freedom. Here we examine their connection in the reverse direction. Does a change in the degree of intellectual freedom have effects upon economic freedom? This relationship is complementary; an increase in intellectual freedom promotes economic freedom as well. The justification for drawing such a connection is based on the argument made in chapter 4 that freedom to act must be construed as freedom to act purposively. To be able to act capriciously or willfully may be what a romantic means by freedom, but the economist who dilates upon the role that markets play in economic organization and the allocation of scarce production resources is talking about man as a rational being, one who considers the probable consequences of his actions. To be able to exercise reason, however, requires more than the possession of a reasoning faculty. One must have empirical knowledge that is relevant to the issue at hand. If a consumer is "free" (in the restricted sense of not being constrained) to spend his income as he wishes, but knows nothing at all about the goods and services which are offered for sale, he is in no more command of his life than if someone else were to determine what he should eat and wear, where he should live, etc. No good argument can be based on extreme imaginary cases; I use this illustration merely to point out that the exercise of economic freedom requires possession of relevant information.

The essentials of this issue have long been recognized by the law in its prohibition of fraud. If an article is offered for sale with false claims, this is considered to be grounds for civil and even criminal action against the seller. Most people would grant that fraudulent claims reduce the welfare of consumers by making their allocation of income less efficient than it might be. I would go further and argue that such practices constrict economic freedom by reducing one's ability to act purposively. The need for information, however, involves more than merely being protected against misinformation. Many of the goods and services that people buy are technically complex, and personal experience cannot always be relied upon to furnish the requisite information. The consumer can easily try different brands of soap until he finds the one that suits him best. (In such cases even the false claims of advertisers is of little moment). But he cannot try out different surgeons in order to build up his knowledge. The patient who has no access to inside information about the qualities of surgeons is forced to buy a pig in a poke. And it is a poke whose cover is kept firmly closed by the medical profession itself, by prohibiting its members from disseminating information about themselves and their colleagues and by attacking others who seek to provide such information. An extension of intellectual freedom in this area, that is, more freedom of inquiry into the quality of medical practice furnished by particular practitioners and more dissemination of such information, would add to the ability of consumers to make rational choices.

The same argument can be made about other professions, including my own. It is not easy to determine what information a student should have to enable him to exercise freedom of purposive choice, but there is no justification for practices that restrict the information that is made available to him. This argument applies also to goods that are offered for sale as well as to services, especially those goods that are technically complex and are infrequently purchased, such as household appliances. At one time the publication of quality information concerning such products was considered ground for civil action, but it now seems plain that there is no warrant for such restrictions on intellectual freedom. In recent years the state itself has entered this area by requiring the testing of products and the publication of information, such as the gas consumption performance of automobiles. This development is not necessarily a pure gain since there is a tendency for those who possess governmental powers to act paternalistically, prohibiting what they disapprove of or consider to be inimical to the people's welfare instead of informing them so that they can make better judgments for themselves. Such prohibitions diminish rather than add to the consumer's freedom of choice. But if the state can provide reliable information, promote the efforts of others to provide information, and prohibit actions that prevent the acquisition and dissemination of information, then economic freedom is enlarged by increasing the scope of those intellectual freedoms which are complementary to it.

Political Freedom as Consequent [+]

The role that intellectual freedom plays in the exercise of political freedom has received so much attention, both in scholarly and vernacular discussion, that it is not necessary to examine it extensively here. The ability to participate in the processes by which collective decisions are made depends upon the right to stand for public office and to vote, but this would be a severely stunted right if it did not also include freedom of discussion. Political freedom must be continuously exercised, not only on one day every two, or four, or six years. The modern theory of collective decision making has improved our understanding of political processes by shedding light on the behavior of different types of decision-making procedures, but its picture of the political process of democratic states leaves the largest part of the canvas blank, since it does not include any delineation of the vital role that open discussion plays in the formation of public opinion. Rational persons may always vote according to their personal interests, but what policies serve these interests is not always, or even often, a plain and simple matter, so there is much room for debate about public policy even when each voter's personal interests are taken as given. In addition, there is a large range of public issues, such as foreign policy, general fiscal policy, and monetary policy, where the connection with one's personal interest is not definable and the debate concerning them revolves instead around conceptions of the "public" interst. Lord Bryce once defined democracy as "government by discussion," which is a penetrating observation of the fact that intellectual freedom is a complement of, indeed an *essential* complement of, political freedom.

The effect of intellectual freedom upon political freedom, however, may under certain special conditions be negative. If intellectual freedom is totally unconstrained, it can be exercised by those who are opposed to political freedom as well as by those who value it. Intellectual freedom can be employed to promote the contention that political freedom should be restricted to a subsector of the populace, such as the dominant racial group, which may even be a minority, as in South Africa. The convinced democrat will regard such restrictions on political freedom as undesirable; must he also seek to prohibit free speech on the part of those who argue for them? This is a difficult question upon which even sincere democrats hold divergent views. My own view, as stated above, is that intellectual freedom must include freedom of expression of opinions that one regards as wrong, evil, or dangerous. Otherwise, intellectual freedom is inevitably confined to the expression of views that are favored by those who control the power of the state.

Are there no cases where the unlimited exercise of intellectual freedom conflicts with the exercise of political freedom? There is one that cannot easily be resolved: when freedom of speech is employed, in a democratic polity, to argue for a general and irrevocable end to political freedom. In every democratic society there are, and always will be, those who seek to replace the system of political freedom by dictatorship. What degree of freedom of speech should be allowed to them? As long as this group is small and there is little possibility that they will actually achieve their aims, there seems to be no warrant for restricting their freedom of speech, assembly, candidature for office, etc. But can the same stance be maintained when such a group grows large and moves close to the assumption of political power? If our answer to this is no, we are saying, in effect, that the enemies of democracy may enjoy intellectual freedom, but only so long as they can do little with it; which seems to place them in the same status as the girl in the old song whose parents permitted her to go swimming provided that she did not go near the water. This is an exceedingly difficult problem, and it may well be a practical one in France and Italy at the present time where there are popular political parties whose counterparts in other countries have proved to be implacable enemies of political freedom. I do not place a minus sign at the head of this section because this does not seem to me to be a problem of importance in the United States.

Justice as Consequent [+]
The effect of intellectual freedom on justice is here noted as unambiguously complementary. This requires some defense since one cannot assume that men will only employ their intellectual freedom to discover truth and to disseminate it, or even that truth invariably leads to actions that are compatible with justice. Should freedom of inquiry be closed to those who wish to investigate matters that are felt to pose potential dangers to the promotion, say, of equality? This matter has come sharply to the fore in recent years with the publication of E. O. Wilson's *Sociobiology*, some of his critics

fiercely contending that it is impermissible to investigate whether human behavior may be genetically determined, because it is inimical to the higher value of equality to conclude from such an investigation that genetic factors may have any influence at all on behavior. Since such types of scientific research cannot have any good consequences and may have some bad ones, they should be proscribed—so goes the argument, which some biologists have used to attack virtually all research into human genetics. Should William Shockley be permitted to speak in public on the subject of racial differences in "intelligence"? A few years ago he was prevented from speaking on a number of university campuses by those who regarded his views as abhorrent and of pernicious effect on the promotion of racial equality.

These are issues that cannot be resolved by simply defending intellectual freedom as a first principle. Many of those who have defended Wilson's right to do research and Shockley's right to speak (and the rights of others to listen if they wish) have so stated their case, but this is weak ground. One person may contend that intellectual freedom is the first principle while another might contend, with equal conviction, that equality is; the argument then becomes one of trying to determine the moral lexicographical order of such things, which cannot advance much beyond the assertion of one's own moral preferences. The debate degenerates into assertion and counterassertion, punctuated invariably by ad hominem argument replete with genetic fallacy.

Can we, instead, say anything of an empirical nature about the relationship between intellectual freedom and justice? In broad terms it seems clear that societies that have restricted intellectual freedom are not noteworthy as ones that have achieved high levels of justice. Such levels may

not be high enough in free societies either, but in any comparative ranking they are clearly superior. Moreover, this is
not an inexplicable empirical phenomenon; the reasons for
it are fairly clear. Justice is a complex primary good with
various, and not necessarily harmonious, specifications, so it
is necessary in practical cases to construct arguments that
focus upon the particular issues at hand. But arguments remain shallow when they are not disputed, so even those who
are right require the challenge of criticism. In his great essay
On Liberty, John Stuart Mill contended that intellectual freedom is required not only to find the truth but, even when it
is already known, to keep it from degenerating into a dead
dogma. The promotion of justice, or any other complex social good, requires intellectual competition, which cannot be
restricted to those who are considered (by whom?) to be
"right-thinking" without seriously undermining the whole
edifice of reason. Even if all social issues could be reduced to
scientific problems, which they cannot, intellectual competition would be necessary since no science can be made
wholly objective, and the social sciences less so than the natural ones.[4]

Anyone who abhors such palpable injustices as racial
discrimination winces when he hears a Shockley discourse
upon the I.Q.s of blacks. But the urge to silence him is not
based upon the desire to save oneself from exposure to bigotry; one could easily achieve that by not going to the lecture or by turning off the television set. What really concerns
one is the possibility that such expressions may affect the
views *of others*. This is the fundamental problem of censorship in general. The censor should examine what he is to
censor. If it tends to corrupt those who are exposed to it,
how does he avoid such effects himself? He can do so by *not*

examining the material, relying instead on hearsay or some other indirect evidence, but that is not supportable as a procedure, though it has frequently been practiced. The only other way is to establish as censors men who are less corruptable than common men. Those who feel that a Shockley should be silenced and who act to silence him elevate themselves to such an elite, superior to ordinary men in their ability to determine what should be read and heard. One need not argue that *anything* may be said in public. Laws of libel and slander are not improper, and I do not think it would be improper to extend them to cover statements made about religious, racial, or other groups, if done with care. But it is one thing to contend that a person must be accountable for what he does, including what he says or writes, and another to prevent him directly from doing it.

Am I arguing here that public statements such as denigrations of members of particular racial groups can never lead to unjust actions against them? To contend that would be to close one's eyes to some of the most monstrous injustices of human history. When the populace is gripped by apocalyptic fear, the suggestion that the Jews are spreading bubonic plague or that the Japanese on the West Coast of North America are preparing to assist an invader may act as potent derangers of an unstable equilibrium. But this does not serve as an argument against intellectual freedom; it leads one instead to recognize that the exercise of it requires that men are calm enough to listen to argument. No rational process can be pursued in the heat of passion; men do not engage in an intellectual activity when they wave banners or shout slogans; the competition of ideas is not a war of ideals. Thus defined, intellectual freedom can be regarded as complementary to the promotion of justice and, as I shall argue presently, to the promotion of welfare as well.

Welfare as Consequent [+]

Intellectual freedom contributes to welfare in an unambiguous way, leaving out of account the problem of whether it can safely be extended to disciples of authoritarian ideologies. Cultural welfare, as discussed in chapter 2, is obviously heavily dependent upon the existence of intellectual freedom and, unless one adopts the view that some people know what is best for the cultural welfare of others better than those others do themselves, the complementarity between them is without limit. Material welfare too is promoted by intellectual freedom since it is necessary to be informed about products and their characteristics if one is to make good choices in the market place. In a more dynamic context, it is plain that the growth of material welfare is heavily dependent upon increase in scientific knowledge about both natural and social phenomena, and it is difficult to believe that this requires restriction upon freedom of inquiry and freedom of debate. It may be that some forms of scientific research endanger welfare, as has recently been argued concerning recombinant DNA research in molecular biology. If this is so it may call for the recognition of a conflictual relationship, confined to very specific areas of scientific inquiry. Some people try to extend this argument to a wider area, calling for constraints upon research into such things as the possible genetic transmission of something called intelligence and even to areas of psychological or social research. This argument however is not based on the possibility that the research procedures may be dangerous in themselves, but on the view that their findings may be misapplied (which is really an argument for constraints on economic and political freedom) or on the view that they may mislead the gullible. Concerning the latter argument one need only point out that there is no evidencé that gullibility is so definitely locatable as to offer a sure guide as to who needs protection from being misled and who can be trusted to be the protector; open debate seems to offer a more reliable corrective.

Political Freedom as Causal Variable

Economic Freedom as Consequent [+]

In recent years much attention has been given to the extent to which freedom to engage in voluntary exchange is restricted by law and regulations in democratic states. It is obviously not possible to contend that a regime of political freedom guarantees that restrictions on economic freedom will be limited to those that are justified by the kinds of considerations noted in the section Economic Freedom as Causal Variable above. But the issue that we have to consider here is not whether wide opportunities for political participation perfectly protect the legitimate exercise of economic freedom, but whether the narrowing of such opportunities would do this better. I see no reason for believing this to be so. On the contrary, it is predictable that when participation in politics is restricted, those who have the ability to exercise political power will use it to promote their own interests and preferences, restricting the economic freedom of others when that is serviceable to themselves. This argument applies, of course, not only to the state but to other organizations as well. A labor union that controls working opportunities for which there are few alternatives has power to restrict the economic freedom of those under its jurisdiction. Its exercise of such power may be improper even if its officers are elected by democratic processes, but it is more likely to be improper if they are not.

Intellectual Freedom as Consequent [+]
In societies where the degree of political freedom is very low it is unlikely that those who wield political power will permit others to enjoy much freedom of speech, assembly, etc. But I am not arguing here on the basis of extreme cases, so the issue is whether further extension of political freedom in societies that are already democratic can be expected to produce effects on intellectual freedom. The main argument which justifies the assertion of complementarity here is based on the fact that societies are not homogenous in terms of race, sex, or other characteristics. If subsections of the population, such as women or blacks, are not permitted to be full participants in the political process they are not likely to have as much opportunity to engage in intellectual activities as those who are, since these opportunities are greatly dependent upon political power. In those areas of the United States where blacks did not have the vote and were otherwise proscribed from political participation, their schooling (provided from the public purse) was inferior, and this alone was sufficient to stunt their exercise of intellectual freedom. Those in the civil rights movement who perceived that an increase in political power by blacks would bring gains in other directions were on sound ground, as the em-

pirical experience of recent years has shown. Racial discrimination, or sexual discrimination, will not be totally eliminated by the extension of political freedom; bigotry and prejudice are too deeply entrenched to be destroyed so simply; but it seems reasonable to expect that further increases in political participation by hitherto repressed groups will act as a complement to intellectual participation as well.

Justice as Consequent [+]

The arguments made in the section above dealing with the effect of intellectual freedom on justice apply with equal weight to the effect of political freedom on justice, so it is not necessary to repeat them in detail. An authoritarian might contend that the achievement of justice requires restriction of political freedom, but this, in effect, assumes that what is just is firmly and finally known, and known only by the few. If this view is rejected, it means not only that intellectual freedom is a complement of justice but that political freedom is also necessary to its effective promotion. The debate over justice cannot be confined to an area that is insulated from politics (academic philosophy, say, or theology, or technical welfare economics). The vernacular discussion may be less sophisticated than the academic one, but there is no warrant for the view that justice is reduced by wide participation in political processes. In the early nineteenth century, when democracy was a new form of political organization, some observers expected that it would lead to the tyranny of the majority with injustice to minority groups. Experience since then suggests that the welfare and rights of minorities are furthered by their ability to participate in political processes even when they do not have the numerical power to determine its decisions. Accordingly, political freedom may be regarded as unambiguously complementary to justice.

Welfare as Consequent [+]

Political freedom is connected with welfare in important ways, most of which have already been noted in the preceding discussion. The political process establishes the framework of laws and the administration of them, which constrain the actions of individuals. Liberal political philosophers have long argued that the welfare of the citizenry is best promoted by a political process in which they are free to participate and this appears to be verified by historical experience. Benevolent dictatorship is not inconceivable a priori, but it is as improbable as the unicorn in real life, and there is no good evidence to suggest that lesser restrictions on political freedom such as, say, confining it to the educated or the well-born, or to the members of "the party," makes for a better system of laws.

The legal framework is only one of the many "public goods" which, for various reasons, must be provided by the political system rather than by voluntary market exchange. Just as the efficient production of private goods requires an information transmittal system between consumers and producers, so does the efficient production of public goods. Politics cannot perform this function for public goods as well as markets do for private ones, but a political system based on open participation is more likely to do better than one that is closed or seriously constrained. For these reasons, it does not seem that any restriction of political freedom is necessary in the interest of promoting welfare; the relationship between them is unambiguously complementary.

Justice as Causal Variable

Economic Freedom as Consequent [−]

The arguments made above with respect to the impact of economic freedom on justice apply with equal weight in the reverse direction. For the same reasons that the promotion of justice requires restrictions on economic freedom, the exercise of economic freedom will be reduced by policies that seek to achieve more equality, equality of opportunity, better provision for need, and fairness of exchange. These arguments need not be repeated here, but it is worth noting that a great deal of the complexity that characterizes the discussion of justice in a capitalistic market economy is due to the mutual interrelationship that exists between economic freedom and justice. The doctrinaire socialist argues that if we destroy capitalism a regime of justice will follow as they day follows night, by the working of natural laws. The doctrinaire libertarian argues with equal confidence that if we give unlimited scope to economic freedom, we will create a world of perfect justice. We have good reason to doubt both of these prescriptions for Edenic restoration. In the real world justice and economic freedom are in conflict and there is no way of avoiding the hard problem of compromise.

Intellectual Freedom as Consequent [+]

In societies such as that of the United States, marginal changes in the satisfaction of most of the justice criteria described in chapter 3 would not have much effect, either positively or negatively, on the amount of intellectual freedom, but one of those criteria is important enough in this connection to be noted. Since I am defining freedom as the ability to engage in purposeful activity as well as the simple absence of constraint, it seems clear that the exercise of intellectual freedom is dependent upon the acquisition of education and the ability to enter intellectual occupations or otherwise engage in intellectual pursuits. Increasing equality of opportunity by reducing social, sexual, and other forms of discrimination in occupations and a general widening of educational opportunities contribute to intellectual freedom to a degree that is not of negligible significance. In this respect, justice is complementary to intellectual freedom.

Political Freedom as Consequent [+]
The same considerations noted directly above apply here as well. In a society where racial and other irrelevant discriminatory practices are substantial, the reduction of them by increasing equality of opportunity in educational and occupations widens the opportunity to participate in political processes.

Welfare as Consequent [+ and −]
As the notation indicates, the effect of justice upon welfare is complementary in some respects and conflictual in others. The criterion of equality of opportunity is powerfully complementary to welfare since it is necessary to the efficient use of human productive resources. All societies have customs, rules, and educational systems that produce barriers to the optimum use of talent and ability. Irrelevant discriminatory practices based on sex, race, linguistic accents, or class status greatly reduce the efficiency with which society makes use of its human resources. People are separated into "noncompeting groups" at early ages when they acquire ed-

ucation and training, and later they face "segmented labor markets" that restrict the free flow of human resources into occupations and prevent their efficient allocation. Breaking down these barriers by widening educational opportunities and reducing discrimination is justified in itself by an important justice criterion, but it also contributes to general welfare as well.

The negative effects on welfare of policies that are aimed at promoting justice arise from carrying equality of income and provision for need to the point where disincentives to effort are produced. Erosion of the connection between work and reward is likely, if carried very far, to impair the economic welfare of a society. This issue need not be elaborated here since it has already been discussed. The minus sign appended to the heading of this section indicates that, in my opinion at least, such a conflict between justice and welfare is not of negligible importance in the United States at the present time.

Welfare as Causal Variable

If we were considering here not incremental changes in economically developed democratic states but discrete differences between very different societies, it could be argued that welfare acts as a complement to freedom. In economically poor societies, where productive capital consists largely of land, the variety of economic opportunities is largely limited to the occupations that are associated with farming and mining. People whose talents and inclinations are differently oriented have little opportunity to exercise them and in this sense one cay say that the level of economic freedom is low. In addition, the historic record shows that such societies are likely to be characterized by high concentration of both wealth and political power, so opportunities to engage in intellectual pursuits and to participate in political processes are restricted to a small sector of the population. In the large view, it would be a great mistake to neglect the contribution that economic development has made to the enlargement of freedom by creating much more diverse forms of wealth in the form of material and human capital, and by its tendency to produce a wider distribution of them.

But the object of this chapter is to examine the cause and consequent relationships among social goods on a much narrower scale, considering only incremental changes for societies such as the contemporary United States. On such a scale, it does not seem to me that any clear relationships, either of complementarity or conflict, exist between changes in welfare considered as causal variable and the three categories of freedom as consequents. No important changes in economic, intellectual, or political freedom can be predicted to flow from incremental changes in welfare, so I do not include here any consequential considerations for relationships such as given in with the preceding sections of this chapter. The effects of incremental welfare changes on justice are, however, important.

Justice as Consequent [+]

The main factor that causes incremental changes in the general level of material welfare in a developed economy is unemployment. Considered in terms of aggregate production of goods and services the fluctuations of economic activity which have occurred in the United States since World War II are small. At no time in this period has actual production fallen short of potential (full employment) production by as much as 10 precent, normally being a great deal smaller. Even a 10 percent slack in the economy amounts to an aggregate output loss which is the equivalent of only about four years of normal growth in productivity. Thus, if the American economy were to experience unemployment sufficiently large to make actual production 10 percent less than potential production *persistently*, year after year, it would mean that the aggregate actual economic welfare as measured by the national income would be persistently four years behind what it could be. That is to say, for example, the national income of 1984 could be achieved in 1980 if there were full employment in 1980; the national income of 1985 could be achieved in 1981; and so on.

This hardly seems like an important problem for a society whose level of material welfare is as high as that of the United States. But that is not the core of the problem at all. The *aggregate* production of goods and services may be only marginally affected by the amounts of unemployment experienced since World War II, but the *distribution* of that aggregate is a different matter. When the unemployment rate is X percent, this does not mean that everyone in the labor force finds that he can sell X percent fewer hours of labor than he wishes or that everyone's income is X percent lower than it would be if there were full employment. Even at an unemployment rate of 10 percent, most people are working full time but some others are not working at all; most people's incomes are as high as they would be at full employment but some are depressed to zero, or to the level sustained by unemployment benefits or other forms of poverty amelioration. The fundamental problem of unemployment is that the distribution of its burdens is highly concentrated upon those members of society who are, typically, among the least able to bear them because they lack any source of income other than the daily sale of their labor. Unemployment is a clear offense against the justice criteria of equality, equality of opportunity, and need, in addition to being, in itself, a wastage of welfare-augmenting productive resources.

Combination of the Relationships

Having completed the examination, pair by pair, of the five social goods in their effects on one another, we can now make some more general assessments by putting our findings together. This is done in the accompanying table. The five goods are listed horizontally as causal variables and vertically as consequential ones. The plus and minus signs in the boxes of the matrix indicate the relationships of complementarity and conflict, respectively, which have been elucidated by the pair-by-pair examinations. A general assessment of each social good can be made by reading the vertical columns of the table.

RELATIONSHIPS AMONG SOCIAL GOODS:
Complementarity = +; Conflict = −

CONSEQUENTIAL VARIABLES	CAUSAL VARIABLES				
	Economic Freedom	Intellectual Freedom	Political Freedom	Justice	Welfare
Economic freedom		+	+	−	
Intellectual freedom	−		+	+	
Political freedom	+/−	+		+	
Justice	+/−	+	+		+
Welfare	+/−	+	+	+/−	

The most important conclusion which emerges from this table is the unambiguous status of intellectual and political freedom. Except for the threat posed by the extension of full intellectual freedom to the ideological enemies of political freedom (which is an immediate problem in some democratic societies but not in the United States) these freedoms are not only good in themselves but they do not have to be constrained in the interest of enlarging any of the other social goods and, indeed, an increase of them has important beneficial effects on all of the others. The analysis shows therefore that there is a sound basis for the emphasis upon intellectual and political freedom in Western political thought. This does not have to depend upon any contention of lexicographical moral priority or natural rights, nor does it rest upon the kind of argument made by Hayek that giving up small amounts of freedom leads one down the road to serfdom where all of it is lost. The defense of the Western tradition can be based on more secure, empirical, foundations.

The status of welfare is also that of an unambiguous good, as the table shows. It requires no restriction, and an increase in it also contributes to important dimensions of distributive justice. The claim of some social critics that the "quality of life" is being eroded in modern society is sometimes used to support the contention that we should constrain and even reverse our demand for material progress. This is erroneous. To increase the quality of life means having more of the things that contribute to it, and this requires rationality and the exercise of good taste, not a general rejection of material improvement. The argument about the quality of life amounts, in effect, to a recognition of the contribution that intellectual freedom can make to the growth of welfare in the broader sense of that term.

The status of justice is much less simple. The enlargement of it contributes to the quantity of other goods, but it also conflicts with economic freedom and welfare in important ways. As the above discussion indicates, these conflicts are mainly due to the fact that justice is an exceedingly complex good in itself. The concept of justice embraces a number of different criteria which are not harmonious with each other. The attempts of modern writers such as Rawls, Nozick, and Buchanan to base a political philosophy upon a homogeneous concept of justice result in untenable simplifications. The idea of justice looms so large in Western social and ethical philosophy that it is understandable why some thinkers regard an answer to the question "What is justice?" to be a prerequisite to all political philosophy. That question, however, has more than one answer; conflict is unavoidable; and the essential problem of politics is one of making tentative assessments and compromises.

As the table shows, economic freedom emerges as the most ambiguous of the five goods from our examination of complementarity and conflict relations. Unless one adopts a natural rights approach to property and a purely commutative theory of justice (both of which are difficult to sustain as exclusively valid criteria even in a simplified analysis), economic freedom is the most instrumental of the goods we have been examining, its main merit deriving from the contribution it makes to the attainment of other things which are good. This contribution is very large, especially because of the role that free market exchange plays in relieving the political system from being unnecessarily overburdened, and because of its effectiveness in raising standards of welfare by contributing to the efficient allocation of scarce productive resources. It is possible that an efficient economy (of a sort) could exist without widespread use of the market mechanism if political freedom were severely restricted; it is possible that a regime of political freedom could exist without the existence of such a market mechanism, but it could not be economically efficient. To have an efficient economy *and* a regime of political freedom, without an extensive market mechanism, is not possible.

In the regions of our functional relationships that are relevant for contemporary democratic societies the marginal contribution that can result from the extension of economic freedom in certain areas is positive, since it seems clear that in most of these societies the state is already overburdened and substantial inefficiencies result from various policies that reduce the operations of markets. But it is also quite clear that restrictions on economic freedom in other areas is necessary in order to promote intellectual and political freedom, welfare, and justice, in ways described above. Some (perhaps many) policies that involve restrictions on the operations of markets may be misguided, deriving either from a doctrinal hostility to the market mechanism or from erroneous empirical or theoretical analysis, but they cannot be condemned on general principle. Some political philosophers, such as Milton Friedman and F. A. Hayek, have attempted to establish economic freedom as the central principle of social policy, but even their own writings admit the existence of conflictual relationships which undermine this position very considerably. Anarchists like Murray Rothbard and Ayn Rand or semi-anarchists like Robert Nozick succeed in supporting the central position of economic freedom only by picturing a society that is irrelevantly different from contemporary reality. Some of the arguments for restriction of economic freedom that are prominent in vernacular politics may be faulty, and in the aggregate they may be excessive, but the attempt to reject them on general principle is a mere doctrinaire faith itself, without secure empirical and theoretical foundations.

The status of economic freedom in this analysis has very little to do with "capitalism," if that term is taken to refer, not to the organization of economic processes by competitive markets, but to the ownership of nonhuman capital by individual persons or collective private entities such as corporations. Most of the arguments made above for the restriction of economic freedom would apply also to a society in which such capital was owned by cooperative associations, labor unions, other types of workers' associations, pension funds, or governments, and some of them would have greater weight. The various forms of market failure would still exist; it would still be necessary to redistribute income in order to ameliorate need; and it would still be necessary to constrain any efforts of such entities to acquire monopoly power, to restrict the intellectual or political freedom of individual persons, or to exercise undue influence over legislatures and courts. Changing the ownership locus of the means of production would not introduce a regime of ubiquitous harmony. Conflictual problems with respect to economic freedom would continue to exist. So what is required is neither a new ideology (or an old one) of socialism, nor a renewal of faith in the virtues of capitalism and free markets, but more detailed analysis of complementarity and conflict among social goods.

Six
The Distribution and Control of Coercive Power

The State, and Other Institutions, as Coercers

POLITICAL FREEDOM IS a necessary constituent of a good society, and, since it is fully congruent with other freedoms and with other social goods (except for the special case of antifreedom parties), there is no need to restrict it in the interest of other worthy objectives; but political freedom is not sufficient, by itself, to guarantee that a society will be well governed. In fact, the existence of a large measure of political freedom tends to obscure the most essential characteristic of all government, the exercise of coercive power. In a dictatorship this feature of government is quite plain, but the existence of democratic political institutions and the establishment of open opportunities for political participation tend to create the illusion that, in such societies, men "govern themselves" in a literal sense—that what the state does in enacting a law is identical to the taking of a New Year's resolution by a single individual to modify his own behavior. All political government is, however, the government of some individuals by others and this is not essentially altered by the widening of political participation. Even if all aspects of power and influence were equally distributed, no action of government could be regarded as literal self-government unless it was derived from the unanimous assent of all those persons, both present and future, who are affected by it. Anything short of this involves coercion of some by others. In democratic societies, majorities, normally of representatives, not of the people themselves,[1] pass laws and establish bureaucracies to implement them. It is possible for government to be *of* the people and *for* the people, but it can never be government *by* the people.

The state is the sovereign repository of power, but it does not enjoy a complete monopoly over the exercise of coercion, even in the most totalitarian order. Personal freedom is constrained not only by law but by custom and practice. If the mores of a society are strongly against the wearing of beards and beads, then some people who would otherwise do so will not, and those who do will be forced to pay for their idiosyncrasy in various ways. If business firms require that executive employees must join a golf club, those who dislike the game and its associated activities are restricted in their freedom if the practice becomes so general that there are effectively no openings for their executive talents which do not carry this condition. Families have great powers of coercion over their young members and, in some families, this does not diminish much when the young reach maturity.

Some actions of the state are clearly aimed at increasing the freedom of some by constraining the freedom of others to coerce them. A policeman walking a beat constrains the freedom of muggers to coerce others. If a government uses tax funds (a coerced payment) to operate a refuge center to which women may go who are in danger of maltreatment by their husbands, then clearly the coercion of the state is being used to reduce other infringements on freedom. If, as in the American South until recent years, racial discrimination operates largely through custom, the enactment of laws that prohibit the continuance of such practices (and attack the mores that sanction them) constrains the freedom to limit freedom.

In some parts of rural England in the last century it was a common custom for people to express their distaste of anyone who was believed to have committed offenses against conventional standards of moral conduct by parading outside his home at night playing "rough music," that is, making as much noise as possible with drums, horns, and other cacophonous instruments. The police would not interfere if the presumed offender was not explicitly identified and the practice was not continued for more than a few nights.[2] They presumably did not worry about the disturbance of the peace of other inhabitants of the house or of nearby residents. In England and America in the eighteenth century, a common penalty for minor offenses was to sentence the offender to sit in the stocks for a few hours. But this did not necessarily mean that he would emerge only with a humbled mien and stiff joints, for in many cases the law, or its administration, regarded a person in the stocks as deprived of civil rights and hence he was a legitimate object of assault by others. The taste for riskless and/or righteous violence on the part of some was great enough to assure that he would complete his sentence fearfully injured, or dead. Placing a price on a man's head "dead or alive" is no mere fiscal policy, since it lifts the normal constraints against the commission of murder. Permitting one person to challenge another to a duel which the latter cannot decline without severe loss of social status constitutes a great restriction on his freedom, by exposing him to the barbarity of his fellows. The necessary use of the coercive power of the state to prevent personal coercion is obvious and has long been a major objective of law.

The state is not the only association that embraces private persons. A great many human activities are carried on through less comprehensive associations of various kinds: labor unions, business firms, churches, clubs, etc. The members of these are constrained in their actions by the rules of their associations, and some of the coercive power of the state often bears upon them only indirectly, through its effect on their associations. A great deal of confusion has been produced by the development of corporate law, which construes the associational entity as a person and applies ordinary common and civil law to it, instead of developing a separate body of associational law which would bear on all associations. The effect of this is that the definition of a person's status vis-à-vis an association of which he is a member is muddied in contemporary jurisprudence. Not only can a person use an association to protect himself from bearing full responsibility for his acts, but he can be constrained in his freedom of action by associational rules, so his power to coerce and his exposure to coercion may both be increased. The radical anarchist is probably right in regarding all associations as having the effect of reducing the total quantity of freedom, in its negative definition, though it does not follow that associations must therefore be destroyed. Man is a club-forming animal for reasons that run far beyond his desire to coerce others, but that makes it all the more necessary to consider the full consequences of this aspect of his behavior.

The coercive power of an institution is inversely related to the alternatives that are available. A business firm can make whatever rules it pleases concerning the behavior of its employees but, if there are many alternative employers, and the labor market generally is characterized by low unemployment, there is a way of escape for anyone who finds the rules oppressive. The reason why the potential coercive power of the family is great is that one cannot shop around for alternatives—the range of choice is very sharply restricted. The existence of a centrally organized universal church is a locus of great coercive power in societies where church membership is considered vital to one's spiritual life or is pragmatically essential to the pursuit of those economic activities that are necessary to one's material or cultural welfare. Voltaire once remarked that "were there but one religion in England, its despotism would be fearful; were there but two, they would be at each other's throats; but there are thirty, and they live in peace and happiness."[3] Before the Reformation the hierarchy of the Catholic church was able to exercise heavy coercive power through threat of excommunication, which greatly restricted personal freedoms. Its condemnation of usury, though much noted as a restriction on free contracting, was of negligible practical importance since it was not much applied in practice. The increase in personal liberty that has attended the growth of alternative religious institutions in the West, and the reduction of the perceived importance of religion in general, is one of the major liberating developments of modern civilization.

In contemporary society the most important locus of

power, other than the state and the family, lies in those institutions that are able to control access to the economic means of livelihood. If, in order to practice a profession or pursue a trade, a person must be a member in good standing of a specific professional or trade association, then his welfare is vitally dependent upon the rules which that association establishes, and his intellectual and political freedom may be significantly restricted if the association chooses to enact rules which its members must follow in those areas. The nature of such associational rules, how they are determined, and whether they may be contested by appeal to an entity that is outside the association itself, are important issues bearing on the degree of freedom enjoyed by individual persons. Henry Simons viewed "syndicalism" as a more important threat to personal liberty than the extension of state power, for reasons of this sort, and others.[4] Recent developments in Great Britain, the motherland of liberty, indicate with portentous clarity the dangers that lie in the growth in coercive power of labor organizations. Those developments merit some specific discussion.

The (U.K.) Trade Union and Labour Relations (Amendment) Act of 1976[5] prescribes that a union may negotiate a closed shop with the employer, which prohibits him from employing anyone who is not a union member in good standing. The act permits the parties to specify the particular labor union that enjoys this status so it is no longer possible, as it was previously, for an employee to meet the closed shop provision by belonging to another union. This effectively prevents any effort on the part of workers who are dissatisfied with the specified union to organize another. It also limits very severely the ability of the members of the specified union to contest the policies of its executive officers, since such actions may place one's membership in jeopardy and without membership in the union one cannot continue to be employed. If the closed shop agreement embraces all the effective employment opportunities for a particular skill, a person who loses his membership cannot pursue his trade anywhere in the economy. Prior to the Act of 1976 workers could appeal against dismissal from union membership to an "Industrial Tribunal" but under the new legislation appeal lies only to a review body established by the Trades Union Congress, which is the main confederation of labor unions, so in this vital matter the power of the established union officialdom is without effective constraint. The fact that no employer is compelled by law to agree to a closed shop does not provide any substantial barrier to the widespread development of the type of closed shop permitted by the 1976 act since it is not clearly in the interest of employers to resist it in the face of union pressure, which one can expect to be very strong in view of the great interest of union officials in the increased power and security of office which such a closed shop provides.

When this legislation was before Parliament it was pointed out that one of its implications was that it could require all employees of the mass media to be members of the specified union in a closed shop and thus subservient to that union's executive. Newspaper reporters and editors, for example, would retain employment only by remaining members in good standing of a union that would probably be dominated numerically, and in its officialdom, by printers, compositors, and other technical workers, so the appearance in print of criticism of those unions, or of the Trades Union Congress, or of the policies of the Labour party which the congress supports, is very likely to be restricted.

The legislation made no response to this vital argument, so the Act of 1976 must be viewed as placing extraordinary potential power to restrict intellectual and political freedom in the hands of the officers of a nongovernmental association.

That apprehensions concerning these developments are not unwarranted is indicated by the action, or lack of it, of the British government in the case of the London *Times* publication of a summary of an article from the *Index of Censorship* which claimed that the British printers' union was actively preventing the publication of criticism of union practices. The *Times*'s union promptly called a protest strike and shut the paper down. In response to Opposition contentions that the government should protect the editorial freedom of the press, the then Prime Minister James Callaghan responded that this freedom did not include freedom to publish inaccuracies[6]—the standard reply of anyone who values political power higher than intellectual freedom.

A further development of potential significance in the United Kingdom is the report of the Bullock Committee early in 1977 proposing radical changes in the internal organization of British industry which would give workers' representatives 50 percent of the seats on the boards of directors of private firms, upon approval of one-third of each company's employees. These representatives would be chosen by the dominant unions, virtually all of which belong to the Trades Union Congress. The Bullock Committee was, seemingly, fairly constituted: three businessmen, three union leaders, three academicians, and one lawyer. But one of the academicians was, prior to his appointment, an advisor to the T.U.C., another was known to be strongly prounion, and all the labor members were officers of the T.U.C. or its affiliated unions.[7] It is perhaps not irrelevant to note

that the British Labour party is heavily supported by the
T.U.C.

At the present time, only half of the British labor force
belong to unions but 90 percent of the union members
belong to T.U.C. affiliates. Since the T.U.C. unions are the
dominant ones in most major industries it is evident that the
effect of the Trade Union and Labour Relations (Amendment) Act of 1976 will be to increase greatly the power of the
T.U.C., to the point of suppressing other unions, and will
lodge immense coercive powers over union members in the
hands of T.U.C. officials. The Bullock Committee proposals
will extend this power into the area of management. The potential effects on intellectual and political freedom in Britain are already becoming clear. In recent years commenta-
tors on the British economic scene have widely attributed
her problem to an excessive sacrifice of economic efficiency
in the pursuit of distributive justice. This may be so, but it
pales into insignificance in the light of the developments in
power relationships noted above. No nation has yet voted itself into a dictatorship; revolution and coup d'état are the
established methods; but the British seem to be inventing a
new one.

It is obvious then that the state is not the only important locus of coercive power. But, as recent developments in
Britain show, for any other institution to grow monstrous in
power it must bend the state to its service, or capture it. The
state is, after all, the legally sovereign power, and all other
associations are ultimately subservient to it in any functioning constitutional order. Because of this, a great deal of political philosophy, both old and new, is directed at the problem of how to constrain the power of the sovereign.

John Locke, during the great political upheavals of the

seventeenth century, tackled this issue in terms of the delineation of an absolute natural right possessed by all—the right to one's own person. From this he developed his celebrated theory of the right of property based on the proposition that when a man labors he mixes his person with an inanimate substance and thereby makes it his own. Such a natural right approach was later reflected in the American Declaration of Independence, the French Declaration of the Rights of Man and the Citizen, and in the constitutions that were adopted by a number of American states after the formation of the Union. Recently, Robert Nozick has attempted to revive this approach by construing the right to acquisition of property, a vital element in his theory, in terms very similar to Locke's.

A form of the natural rights approach is to rely on the constitutional entrenchment of a Bill of Rights that specifies certain things which the state may not do and, more importantly, that requires that all legislation must conform to certain general requirements. This can be a potent force for the restriction of state power, as the history of American jurisprudence shows, but that history also indicates that such provisions can act to extend state power when the exercise of coercion by other organizations is at issue, so it is not, in principle, a barrier to coercion by the state, as such. There is no natural law that guarantees that when the state acts to constrain the coercive power of other associations it does not produce more coercion than it prevents. Moreover, it is clear that the effectiveness of the bill of rights type of device depends on the characteristics of the rest of the political system. An examination of the constitution of the USSR gives one the impression that Soviet citizens enjoy the greatest degree of freedom from state power of any people in the world. In response to President Carter's campaign on human rights in the early period of his presidency, *Pravda* claimed that the rights of Soviet citizens are "practically unlimited by anything except one demand, namely that enjoyment of these rights by an individual should not be to the detriment of other people and society at large"[8] a mild and reasonable restriction, if one pays no attention to the actual practice.

Natural rights philosophies were out of favor in the nineteenth century due to the influence of utilitarianism. Bentham called such theories "nonsense on stilts." His most important disciple, John Stuart Mill, attempted to solve the problem of limiting the power of the state by demarcating two spheres of action, one purely "self-regarding" and therefore not a legitimate object of state interference. This principle is workable only if such a line of demarcation is locatable and the sphere of self-regarding action it delineates is not negligibly small. Unfortunately, it is not possible to fulfill these requirements. The use of seat belts in automobiles, for example, cannot be described as a purely self-regarding matter since, if the nonuser is injured, other members of his family might suffer, the other clients of insurance companies might have to pay higher premiums, and the state treasury might have to pay for his medical care. Even cases where the action of some persons affects others only by virtue of the latter's disapproval of it, such as homosexuality between consenting adults, cannot be summarily dismissed. The view that actions of the state that are mainly paternalistic ought to be scrutinized with special care and resisted is a sound one, but Mill's demarcation cannot provide a hard rule that prescribes the appropriate limits of state action.

Another formal approach to the problem of the appropriate limits of state action is Paretian welfare economics.

This proceeds on the eminently sensible claim that an action is justified when it produces more good than harm. When the prescription is added however that there must be no interpersonal comparisons of utility, the orbit of legitimate state interference is restricted nearly to zero, for there is hardly any action that harms *no one*. The compensation principle helps to meet this difficulty but, as economists have pointed out, it is necessary not only to show a benefit-cost calculation that demonstrates that full compensation of those harmed would leave positive net benefits, but also to describe a practical procedure by which that compensation could be paid, and this is very difficult.

Restricted by the prohibition against interpersonal comparisons, Paretianism has reference only to that primary social good we have called welfare. The long debate over the distribution of income among Paretian economists is an effort to extend its applicability to justice, with notable lack of success. But even if all these problems could be technically surmounted, there is still a primary social good left out of the calculation: freedom. Only by regarding personal freedom purely as instrumental, as a means to the achievement of welfare and justice, and not as a value in itself, can Paretianism make any case at all.[9] A legitimate complaint against the modern state is that it typically neglects the freedom costs of its actions, focusing too exclusively on welfare and justice, a practice which is supported by Paretianism and perhaps owes something to the great increase in the role of professional economists as policy advisors to governments.

In what direction do we turn then if all efforts to define the legitimate limits of state power fail and effective guarantees are not securely provided by constitutional devices such as a bill of rights? The only recourse is to recognize that freedom can only be protected by a general environment of freedom; that is, it can only preserve *itself*. The problem of preserving and/or promoting freedom is not a matter of establishing hard general principles, but requires an examination of the contemporary condition of a particular society in order to locate the important points at which freedom is endangered, or at which it can be further enlarged. The problem of freedom in the Soviet Union is very different from that in the United States but, in either case, progress can be made only by starting from where one is.

So far as contemporary Western democracies are concerned, the factors that require special attention are of two sorts: those that tend to produce institutional concentrations of coercive power, and those that tend to release the persons who actually wield that power from the necessity of bearing responsibility for their acts.

Power Concentration and The Rule of Law

The "positive" concept of freedom, which focuses upon power to give effect to one's wishes, does not provide a satisfactory vehicle for the discussion of freedom since what one wishes to do as a member of a society usually involves others. Except for the pure case of voluntary and "fair" exchange, power to do what one wishes restricts the power of others to do as they wish and, as we have seen, even a workable regime of fair exchange involves numerous restrictions on what one is permitted to do. For these reasons, and others, it is sometimes useful to construe freedom in negative terms as the absence of constraints on action by the action of others. This serves to direct attention to important considerations: that freedom can never be absolute, that it is a personal condition, and that the constraints upon one person's freedom consist of the power another person has to coerce him.

Some of these constraints may be direct, such as those exercised by superiors over subordinates in any association that is formally organized on a hierarchical scheme, such as a business firm, or in associations that are less explicit hierarchies, such as families.[10] The important constraints on personal freedom, however, are those that are operated through the mediation of associations, for only through associations can large and comprehensive coercive powers be concentrated in a few hands, and associations can, as well, be used to insulate those who wield power from bearing responsibility for their acts. In a society that does not have a powerful established church that is capable of exercising constraints upon intellectual freedom directly through so-called moral pressure, it is in the spheres of political and economic organization that important threats to freedom lie. The dangers are appreciable wherever there are concentrations of power; they are very great when these power concentrations are gathered into a unified organizational center; they are overwhelming when the officers of such an organization can wield power arbitrarily. The old aphorism says "Eternal vigilance is the price of freedom." That vigilance must be directed at developments that tend to concentrate power and exempt those who wield it from personal responsibility.

Human history is, with one great, and so far brief, exception, a story of variations on a single theme: the concentration of both economic and political power, and the close linkage of the two. The exception is the rise of Western capitalism and political democracy during the past few hundred years. Prior to this development, both economic and political power were dependent upon the ownership of land and thus were tightly connected. Landed property was the only significant source of wealth and it was also the basis of participation in political processes. With the growth of industry and commerce in the eighteenth century, new sources of wealth began to arise, challenging the landed power, whose monopoly was first undermined in the economic sphere and then was broken in the political one. The first significant crack in the political sphere appeared in Britain with the Reform Bill of 1832, which began the extension of the franchise.[11] David Hume, who died in that climactic year 1776, has often been described as a "tory" historian, but he was the first to note the significance, and merit, of the effects that the decentralization of economic power were having upon the extension of political freedom, a point that Adam Smith emphasized to the extent of calling these political effects "by far the most important of all" the consequences of the growth of capitalism.[12]

The modern history of the West has led some observers (e.g. Milton Friedman)[13] to draw a connection of necessity, and even sufficiency, from capitalism to freedom, even though it is clear that history is not governed by "laws" of this sort. Paradoxically, these proponents of the primacy of capitalism agree with Marx in regarding economics as basic, and politics as merely part of the superstructure of social relationships, which rests upon the economics in a totally dependent way. To the extent, however, that the defense of capitalism by Friedman and others is aimed at the threat to freedom posed by contemporary Marxism they are on sounder ground, for this latter ideology has become a powerful source of modern views that it is desirable to concentrate economic and political power and to fuse the two together again. Because of this, Marxism offers great attractions to authoritarian political philosophies of widely diverse sorts, whether they are motivated by religious inspiration as in Khadafy's Libya, utopian aspirations to remold mankind as in Castro's Cuba or Pol Pot's Cambodia, or a simple thirst for personal power as in Amin's Uganda. The authoritarian who embraces Marxism, or merely calls himself a Marxist, obtains thereby a powerful legitimization of his power, which he can invoke by no more demanding means than trotting out the established clichés about the "dictatorship of the proletariat," the "class struggle," the exploitative nature of "surplus value," the threat of "imperialism" (of the capitalistic type), and the "laws of historical development." The authoritarian features of Marxism also appeal to some intellectuals who assume that the new centralized society will be a Platonic one; rule will be by the wisest and best, that is to say, by right-thinking intellectuals like themselves;[14] which only demonstrates how ignorant of history, and naive, intellectuals can sometimes be.

The defender of freedom is at a disadvantage in debate with authoritarians, especially Marxist ones, because he must make more complex arguments. In one respect, the defense is a simple one, resting upon Lord Acton's famous dictum that all power corrupts its possessor. No one can be trusted with great power, whether he is an Idi Amin, or a Saint Dominic, or even a Saint Francis. (The role of the Dominican Order in the Holy Inquisition and the Franciscan Order in the conquest of New Spain should stand as a permanent warning against anyone who contends that he wants power only to do good. As Frank Knight once remarked, who ever claimed otherwise?) But the simple proposition that concentration of power is inimical to liberty, sound though it is, in itself helps little to assess the problems of contemporary democratic societies that are not faced with threats of authoritarian political ideologies which are close to achieving political power by constitutional means. In such societies, the relevant intellectual attack on liberty comes not from Marxists or fascists but, perhaps unwittingly, from sources like the disciples of J. K. Galbraith who argue that the economic and political "technostructures" should be hardened and fused together, and by intellectuals like Wassily Leontief who, being modern Comteans, are attracted by the promise of orderliness and efficiency offered by the use of social science as an instrument of economic planning by the state.

A political system that is based on widespread participation is unlikely to concentrate its power to a degree that becomes a serious threat to the preservation of freedom. In the congressional system, great power is lodged in the executive branch and is legitimized by the fact that the president holds office by direct decision of the electorate at large. But every congressman and senator is also a locus of considerable independent power and the courts are not subservient to the executive or to congress, the constitution providing them with power to oppose the will of either. The distribution of power among these branches, and within them, varies a great deal from time to time, but the historical evidence, including the Watergate affair, shows that it is not easy to establish a secure tyranny by concentrating power within the political system itself so long as the electoral process is not subverted and intellectual freedom remains large.

The parliamentary system lacks the same structure of checks and balances and typically does not have constitutionally entrenched limitations on political power, but its history also demonstrates a large ability to maintain a regime of freedom. The failure of Indira Gandhi to subvert the Indian parliamentary system shows that even great efforts to stifle opposition are unavailing so long as free elections are regarded as the only method by which power can be legitimized and the people are not effectively cowed by fear of loss of livelihood or personal safety. When ultimate political power rests in the hands of the people in a system that permits open candidature for office, free discussion, and fair elections, there is a ready remedy for all threats to liberty, since the people can control the sovereign power of the state and use it, if need be, to constrain the misuse of power in other areas. The danger flag flies when forces are at work that transfer the ultimate source of power from the people at large to a restricted subset: "the party," the military class, the police, a religious organization, or an economic oligarchy. All these types of tyranny have been experienced, past and present, by human societies, and there is no reason to believe that any of them is totally irrelevant as a potential danger even in modern Western societies, so the vigilance which is the price of freedom must scan a wide area.

In the later nineteenth century the vernacular vigilance of America was strongly focused upon the growth of economic oligarchy. The subversion of the state by economic power was perceived to pose an immediate threat to democratic government.[15] The antitrust movement was inspired somewhat by early perception of the effect of monopolization on economic efficiency; more by recognition that monopolies offended the justice principle of fair exchange;

but most of all by the fear that concentrated economic power was a threat to political freedom. The corporation was a fairly new form of business organization at that time but it was growing rapidly, and those who were apprehensive about it then would probably not revise their opinions today. The corporation is now the almost universal form of business organization and it has been immensely elaborated by a variety of devices such as subsidiary companies, holding companies, conglomerates, etc. Many observers of the contemporary scene regard it as a major threat to freedom in all of its aspects: economic, political, and intellectual.[16]

Property ownership may[17] be distributed in a highly unequal fashion, but the corporate form permits the pyramiding of its power and the concentration of that power in a few hands to a much greater degree than does the property itself. The control of the modern corporation rests in the hands of a small minority of its legal owners; it may in fact be effectively exercised by its managerial officials who need not be shareholders at all.[18] Moreover, even the legal owners of a corporation may not be those who have provided its capital. When a pension fund, for example, purchases the stock of a corporation, the legal right to exercise the shareholders' power is vested in the trustees of the pension fund, not the people whose contributions have provided the money. Pension funds are the most rapidly growing repositories of financial wealth in America.[19] Their trustees may be banks, insurance companies, labor unions, or ad hoc bodies; whatever the case, it is the trustees who wield the power of wealth, not the pension contributors, and it is not safe to assume that trustees will place the interests of the putative beneficiaries ahead of their own. The disclosures a few years ago of the operations of the Teamster's Union Pension Fund show what great latitude trustees may enjoy to devote such wealth to their own chosen purposes or even to employ it to coerce those who have contributed it. The state is not the only institution that can levy a tax and then use the proceeds to bully the taxpayers in an arbitrary fashion.

The concentration of economic power through the corporate form of business enterprise, the establishment of trusteeships, and the like, are all potent threats to freedom but this power still remains limited, and exposed to effective attack, as long as it does not capture the seat of sovereignty, the state. The use of economic power to corrupt legislative, executive, or judicial officers is a serious danger which is ever present in any society. The outright subjugation of the state by another repository of power is the ultimate danger and is more rare, but not to be dismissed, as recent developments in Great Britain, noted above, indicate. More insidious perhaps is the view that the state should take over other centers of power by nationalizing industry or by instituting detailed and comprehensive "economic planning." In such a symbiosis, however, the dog and his tail are apt to change roles; the democratic state that sets out to capture the other centers of power is very likely to become the captive *of* them, and be destroyed.

The dispersion of power is a necessary but not sufficient condition for the maintenance of personal freedom. Power cannot be dispersed to the point that no one is able to coerce anyone else, as in the anarchistic utopia. All organizations are oligarchic, including those which are ideologically or philosophically opposed to oligarchy,[20] and their senior officials possess coercive power over their subordinates, and over outsiders who are dependent upon the organization's services. Since power inevitably organizes itself into a hierarchical order, an essential element of a free society is that those who occupy the high places in this order be constrained in the exercise of power regardless of how they attain those positions. In the literature of democratic political philosophy this is the doctrine of "the rule of law." That phrase, however, is not as serviceable at it might be because it is subject to various interpretations, some of which are in fact unworkable or undesirable.

One such unacceptable interpretation of the principle of the rule of law is represented by the phrase that a good polity consists of "a government of laws and not of men." This is a very old idea, going back at least to Aristotle, Livy, and Cicero.[21] The sixteenth-century Venetian historian, Gasparo Contarini, attributed the political merits of that remarkable republic to the fact that, unlike other states, it based sovereignty "on laws not men."[22] In revolutionary America the phrase was a popular expression of the idea of liberty, promoted especially, according to one historian, by its specific incorporation into the Massachusetts state constitution of 1780.[23] In modern discussion it still finds extensive employment, for example by Milton Friedman in his defense of the dependence of political freedom on a capitalistic form of economic organization.[24]

As a slogan, the phrase "a government of laws and not of men" is appealing to the defender of freedom but, like most slogans, it has better sound than sense. The plain fact is that there can be no such thing as a government of laws and not of men. All government, in all spheres, is operated by men, not by disembodied "laws" in themselves. Laws, of the kind we are considering, are not only made by men as legislators but interpreted by men as judges and applied by men as administrators. These functions cannot be performed by abstract or mechanical entities, so this version of the principle of the rule of law only serves to direct attention away from the vital problem of controlling those who wield political and social power. Moreover, as a slogan, it is not necessarily the exclusive property of libertarians and identifiable only with the defense of freedom. If it implies that the power of men over men can be eliminated, replaced by political laws that are as detached as the laws of nature, the slogan could easily be adopted by the Saint-Simonian or the Marxist who proclaims the virtues of an ideal state in which government has been replaced by an automatic, though vague, "administration of things."

Another misinterpretation of the rule of law is that its requirements are only fulfilled if those who administer the law apply them indiscriminately, without any interposition of their own judgment, upon all who break them, aiming to emulate the total objectivity of the laws of nature. If the laws of the state were administered in such a fashion, and with equal "success," most of the citizenry would be in jail, since we break laws almost every day of our lives. We jay-walk, neglect to signal for turns, and litter the streets. We engage in libel and slander as a normal part of social inter-course. The best of men are continually engaged in subver-sion, attempting to undermine the political order, whatever it happens to be, and conspiracy is ubiquitous. The hu-maneness of any system of laws is very much dependent upon the use of discretion, and legal progress has often been achieved by simply allowing laws to fall into disuse rather than by explicitly repealing them.

The principle of the rule of law, properly construed, does not mean that laws are automatic or that they are ap-plied "impersonally." It requires that the persons who apply them are themselves subject to the same laws and must bear responsibility for the discretion they employ, and are not protected from this by any claim that they act as *agents* of an associative body such as a corporation, a labor union, or a government. The evil of the Nixon administration, and its downfall, stemmed from its failure to understand the principle of the rule of law in this sense. The senior officials believed that their positions rendered them exempt from the burden of responsibility and when it became plain that they would not be allowed to claim such special status, they attempted instead to conceal their acts. Power may, as another slogan states, corrupt all who possess it, but it is unavoidable in an organized society, so we must find ways to control it. To do so means that it must not be permitted to become concentrated, and wherever it is and however great or small it is, those who wield it must be held accountable for what they do. Lord Acton's famous aphorism would be more incisive if we rephrased it to say: "Power corrupts, and power without responsibility, corrupts absolutely."

In a competitive economy, the agents of a business enterprise are effectively rendered responsible for their acts by competition itself. The threat of bankruptcy is a potent constraint upon arbitrariness. The same applies to other institutions. When alternatives are many, coercion is small. It is possible for a society to maintain a competitive order with respect to its business enterprises, labor associations, religious institutions, educational institutions, etc., and, as I have already stressed, it is vital to the preservation of freedom that efforts to restrict competition in these areas be frustrated. Some degree of competition exists with respect to governments as well and it is not of negligible importance as a brake on coercive power. The United States was populated by people from other lands who came in search of freedom as well as material welfare, people willing to pay the high cost of separation from home and family, loss of linguistic skills, and the sacrifice of property, in return for the promise of liberty. It is evident today that the most repressive states must erect walls to keep their people from escape, as a condition of the effective operation of tyranny.

One could argue from this that the world at large would be a freer place if it were divided into much smaller states with free movement of people and goods among them. The "utopia" part of Robert Nozick's *Anarchy, State, and Utopia* is based on such a view, but it is, unfortunately, as unrealistic and as irrelevant as any other utopia when advanced as a complete solution. A world postulated as consisting of states that allow such freedom of movement is implicitly assumed to be composed of benign and freedom-respecting governments to begin with, which assumes *away* the major part of the problem. Since freedom requires the availability of alternatives, it is not unimportant, even in a democratic society, to provide alternatives of government where this is practical. Federalism does this to a degree in a constitutional fashion and the existence of independent local government extends it further. The recent interest of economists in federalism and other devices that reduce the size of jurisdictions has largely been focused upon the issue of efficiency in the provision of public goods and services, but such devices are also germane to the problem of freedom. In the fairly recent past the issue of "states' rights" in the United States was mainly concerned with the discriminatory coercions that certain states were applying to minority racial groups within their borders, and the federal power was effectively employed against these practices. But the pendulum has now swung to the other side. The superior power of the federal government, most notably its fiscal power, is used today to coerce states and other institutions (such as universities, which are constitutionally within state jurisdictions) to accommodate themselves to federal policies. Next to the power that a state can wield through its police and military and by means of an established church, fiscal power is the most potent weapon of a government and it consists not only of its authority to tax but also of its ability to decide who will be the beneficiaries of public expenditure.

Even if we lived in a world of small states or well-functioning federalisms, however, the preservation of freedom would not be sufficiently guaranteed by such means alone. When the exercise of choice involves moving home and family and seeking a new means of livelihood, the costs are high. Moreover, one cannot assume that the separate states would compete effectively to attract people as business firms do to attract customers, so all states may be alike in the degree of freedom they afford to their citizens. The preservation of liberty therefore requires that governments operate in a regime of political freedom which, in the context of the present discussion, means that their officers must be accountable for their actions. The primary mechanism for achieving this is, of course, that of democratic politics, but this only assures that those who hold office by election are subject to direct personal responsibility. A government consists of much more than a legislature and one, or a few, elected executive officers. It also contains a vast bureaucracy, many members of which wield power of various kinds and are not directly accountable to the people. The coercive powers of those who act as agents of the state in administrative capacities is inevitably large and there is no way of making them fully responsible for their acts, but the defense of freedom requires that they be restricted, as much as possible, in the extent to which they can exercise power arbitrarily. All officials claim to act for the public good, but it is safer to assume that all men, including bureaucrats, heavily discount the welfare of others, and one must try to keep this rate of discount low.

The rule of law is unnecessarily undermined in modern democratic states by two widespread practices: the excessive secrecy of bureaucratic activities and the excessive use of administrative law. It is a long-established democratic principle that legislatures and courts should operate openly. Any tendency to the contrary is immediately perceived as a threat to liberty, a perception encouraged by a free press which, in a practical way, depends upon legislatures and courts for much of its copy. Most men, perhaps all, are prepared to do in secret things that they would fear to do, or be ashamed to do, in public, so the reporting of governmental activities acts as a constraint on arbitrary power by itself. It is also evident that no effective discussion of governmental policies can take place without extensive knowledge of what they are, so the role of intellectual freedom in the promotion of political freedom cannot be played in a regime of secrecy. Moreover, even if what is done openly and what is done secretly were identical, the vernacular perception fears the latter more. The English Court of Star Chamber under the Tudors was arbitrary and vicious to a degree that could hardly be exceeded, but when it was made into a secret tribunal under the Stuarts, the opposition to it increased greatly and led to its abolition. Men fear what they imagine more than what they can see.

In the modern democracy, courts and legislatures do not

operate behind a thick curtain of secrecy, but administrative bodies often do. In the United States, the regulatory agencies such as the Federal Communications Commission or the Federal Reserve operate more openly than in most other countries and the trend is to increase this, but the administrative deliberations of executive departments take place behind the curtain. It would be foolish to argue that all the activities of a government should be open and that the members of the public or the press be free to go wherever they choose and examine whatever documents as suits their pleasure, but issuing a "secret" stamp to every official, without constraints on its use, invites excess of arbitrariness and erosion of the rule of law.

The insulated status of the bureaucrat is greatly increased by the use of administrative law which, in effect, places the real lawmaking power in the hands of the bureaucracy itself. The laws passed by the Congress are often very long and detailed but many of them leave the vital specifics to be determined by administrative regulations. When the enabling legislation passed by the Congress is itself constitutionally valid, the regulations which are constructed under its umbrella are regarded by the courts to have as much authority as legislative law, even though an examination of the congressional debates may disclose that the regulations are at variance with the legislators' intentions.

The excessive use of administrative law in the modern democratic state severely undermines the role of politics. Experts are empowered to make decisions on matters that are not within the proper scope of their technical competence; the foundations are laid thereby for the development of the kind of society which Plato recommended and Auguste Comte espoused, one in which politics has disappeared and, with it, the liberty of the people. In contemporary discussion of the role of economists and other experts in government one often hears the charge that they practice degenerate sciences—political economics, or political biology, or political physics—which are designed to serve the partisan interests of politicians. This is often the case, but more important is the tendency of experts, like other men, to serve their own interests and objectives. Give them the authority to make the law and it is likely that they will make such law as suits their own convenience and enlarges their arbitrary powers. By such a process the public servant becomes the public master.

The vigilance which is the price of liberty is not effectively employed if it is directed at threats to freedom that are more imaginary than real. Abstract philosophizing can construct a long list of policies, practices, and institutional arrangements that are theoretically dangerous, but the capacity for vigilance is limited, and is needlessly dissipated if not directed at those places where it is most needed, which differs in different societies and at different times. The efficient use of any scarce resource requires that it be properly allocated. In some modern democratic states, such as France and Italy, it seems clear that a large part of the supply of vernacular vigilance should be directed at the activities of political parties that embrace ideologies that are opposed to liberty. In Britain the prime contemporary concern should be focused on the growth of labor syndicalism which threatens to turn the state into a submissive captive of its own oligarchy. In most other democratic countries the leading present problem is the growth of bureaucratic structures, both inside and outside the sphere of government, which concentrate power in a few hands not subject to effective constraint either by competition or responsibility. No society protects its liberty by concerning itself with problems that it does not have, so the distribution of vigilance must change with the times, and not lag much behind the march of events which continuously alters the locus of power.

Notes

1. Politics and Value Judgments

1. J. K. Galbraith, *The New Industrial State* (Boston: Houghton Mifflin), 1967.

2. Isaiah Berlin, *Four Essays on Liberty* (Oxford University Press, 1969), p. 118. See also his paper "Does Political Theory Still Exist?" in Peter Laslett and W. G. Runciman, eds., *Philosophy, Politics, and Society* (2d series; Oxford: Blackwell, 1962).

3. Lionel Robbins, *An Essay on the Nature and Significance of Economic Science* (London: Macmillan, 1932).

4. K. J. Arrow, *Social Choice and Individual Values* (New York: Wiley, 1951).

5. Robert Nozick, *Anarchy, State and Utopia* (New York: Basic Books, 1974); James M. Buchanan, *The Limits of Liberty* (Chicago: University of Chicago Press, 1975).

6. For some further discussion see my paper "The New Contractarians," *Journal of Political Economy* (1976). In that paper I represented John Rawls (*A Theory of Justice*, Cambridge: Harvard University Press, 1971), as well as Nozick and Buchanan, as advancing a procedural philosophy. I now realize that such a common labeling is erroneous. Rawls proposes a procedure which, he contends, generates sound moral principles; Nozick and Buchanan claim to have discovered a procedure which, in itself, is moral. It is perhaps a fine point but not unimportant in the discussion of morals.

7. The recent discussion of this as a principle of distributional equity stems from A. P. Lerner, *The Economics of Control* (New York: Macmillan, 1944).

8. The issue of the relationship between facts and values has been de-

bated ever since David Hume, in the mid-eighteenth century, argued that they are matters of fundamentally different kinds, and increasingly so since G. E. Moore, in the early twentieth century, called the attempt to derive values from facts the "naturalistic fallacy." Some modern philosophers have attempted to demonstrate that it is not a fallacy and thus to open the door to a naturalistic methodology of morals. I do not think that this attempt has been the least bit successful, but the issue cannot be discussed fully here. For two statements advancing opposite positions on the matter see J. R. Searle, "How to Derive 'Ought' From 'Is'," *Philosophical Review* (1964), and Anthony Flew, "Evolutionary Ethics," in W. Hudson, ed., *New Studies in Ethics* (New York: St. Martin's Press, 1967).

2. Welfare

1. David Hume, "Of the Populousness of Ancient Nations," *Writings on Economics*, Eugene Rotwein, ed. (Madison: University of Wisconsin Press, 1970).

2. A. C. Pigou, *Work and Welfare* (London: Macmillan, 1912) and *The Economics of Welfare* (London: MacMillan, 1920). Many of the important propositions in welfare economics were stated earlier by Henry Sidgwick, in his *Principles of Political Economy* (London: MacMillan, 1883), but the modern analytical work derives from Pigou.

3. Robert Southey, *Sir Thomas More; or, Colloquies on the Progress and Prospects of Society* (London, 1829); T. B. Macaulay, "Southey's Colloquies" (1830), *Critical and Historical Essays*, Hugh Trevor-Roper, ed. (New York: McGraw-Hill, 1965). The student of the history of ideas will appreciate that I use Southey and Macaulay in the following discussion only as prototypical adversaries, in a long and (apparently) endless debate. For a comprehensive review of this, focusing mainly but not exclusively on the past century, see W. Warren Wagar, *Good Tidings: The Belief in Progress from Darwin to Marcuse* (Bloomington: Indiana University Press, 1972).

4. Tibor Scitovsky, *The Joyless Economy: An Inquiry into Human Satisfaction and Consumer Dissatisfaction* (New York: Oxford University Press, 1976), p. 133.

5. R. G. Evans, "Does Canada Have Too Many Doctors? —Why Nobody Loves an Immigrant Physician," *Canadian Public Policy—Analyses de Politiques* (Spring 1976). See also the Summer, 1977 issue of that journal for discussion of Evans's argument.

6. For a recent review of the evidence, see J. J. Lambin, *Advertising, Competition, and Market Conduct in Oligopoly over Time: An Econometric In-*

vestigation in Western European Countries (Amsterdam: North Holland, 1976).

7. J. K. Galbraith, *The Affluent Society* (Boston: Houghton Mifflin, 1958).

8. Some biologists have recently argued that a natural unit is provided by the extent of shared genetic material in different organic entities. See, for example, Richard Dawkins, *The Selfish Gene* (New York: Oxford University Press, 1976). It is apparent, however, that this can do very little to explain social distance discounting that is based upon cultural differences, and the suggestions of some sociobiologists that genetics holds the key to the explanation of this social phenomenon is, at the least, premature.

9. Richard A. Easterlin, "Does Economic Growth Improve the Human Lot? Some Empiricul Evidence," in Paul A. David and Melvin W. Reder, eds., *Nations and Households in Economic Growth: Essays in Honor of Moses Abramovitz* (Palo Alto, Calif.: Stanford University Press, 1974). See also Fred Hirsch, *Social Limits to Growth* (Cambridge, Mass.: Harvard University Press, 1976).

10. See his essays collected in *The Ethics of Competition and Other Essays* (New York: Kelley, 1935), and *Freedom and Reform: Essays in Economics and Social Philosophy* (New York: Harper, 1947). On the larger theme see J. Huizinga, *Homo Ludens: A Study of the Play Element in Culture* (Boston: Beacon Press, 1950).

11. A. O. Hirschman, *The Passions and the Interests: Political Arguments for Capitalism Before Its Triumph* (Princeton, N.J.: Princeton University Press, 1977).

3. Justice

1. Scott Gordon, "The New Contractarians," *Journal of Political Economy* (1976).

2. David Hume, *Treatise of Human Nature* (1739–40), L. A. Selby-Bigge, ed. (Oxford: Clarendon Press, 1888, 1975), p. 495.

3. A grotesque suggestion for a rule, which for obvious reasons did not enter the vernacular, was that advanced by J. H. von Thünen, the brilliant nineteenth-century precursor of neoclassical economics who, after much complex labor, concluded that the just wage of the laborer is determined by the formula $\sqrt{(ap)}$, where a is the laborer's subsistence requirement and p is the average product of labor. Von Thünen thought so well of this that he ordered that the formula should be carved on his tombstone.

4. For a good critical examination of exchange theory as applied to so-

ciology see Anthony Heath, *Rational Choice and Social Exchange* (New York: Cambridge University Press, 1976). For a briefer examination, contrasting exchange theory with the other major paradigms of sociological theory, see Jonathan H. Turner, *The Structure of Sociological Theory* (Homewood, Ill.: Dorsey Press, 1974).

5. This point is stressed by Arthur M. Okun, *Equality and Efficiency: The Big Tradeoff* (Washington, D.C.: Brookings, 1975).

6. Alice French, *The Lion's Share* (Indianapolis, Ind.: Bobbs-Merrill, 1907).

7. In fact it is now well recognized by economists that marginal productivity theory is, at best, only a theory of factor *price*, not of factor income, much less a theory of personal income. As a normative theory it supplies not a justice principle, but an efficiency theorem: If a factor of production, labor say, is to be allocated between two industries, A and B, it is evident that the allocation is optimal when the marginal product of labor in the two is equal, or $MPL_A = MPL_B$. In a private enterprise economy of profit-maximizing firms, each will equate the marginal product of labor to the wage rate, or $MPL_A = w_A$ and $MPL_B = w_B$. If the "labor" we are talking about is homogeneous and there is perfect competition in the labor market, $w_A = w_B$. The condition of efficient allocation, externalities aside, is met.

8. Jacob Viner, *The Role of Providence in the Social Order: An Essay in Intellectual History* (Philadelphia: American Philosophical Society, 1972), p. 89.

9. M. Paglin, "The Measure and Trend of Inequality: A Basic Revision," *American Economic Review* (1975). See also a number of articles critical of Paglin's procedure in the same journal, 1977.

10. "In the year 400 St. Chrysostom was preaching at Constantinople that the communism of Acts was a practical ideal for Christian communities; he gave facts and figures to prove that everyone in the congregation would be rich if wealth were pooled and he said he hoped this could be done in his own lifetime." Richard Schlatter, *Private Property: The History of an Idea* (London: Allen & Unwin, 1961), p. 39. The data at least have been improved over the past fifteen centuries.

11. See, e.g., T. N. Carver, *Essays in Social Justice* (Cambridge, Mass.: Harvard University Press, 1925). For a less organismic view, see Leslie Stephen, "Social Equality," *International Journal of Ethics*, 1891.

12. See, e.g., J. E. Meade, *Efficiency, Equality and the Ownership of Property* (Cambridge, Mass.: Harvard University Press, 1965); A. P. Lerner, *The Economics of Control* (New York: Macmillan, 1944); and Amartya Sen, *On Economic Equality* (New York: Norton, 1973).

13. See James Tobin, "On Limiting the Domain of Inequality," in E. S.

Phelps, ed., *Economic Justice* (Baltimore, Md.: Penguin, 1973), pp. 447–63, for an excellent discussion of "specific egalitarianism" and different arrangements for accomplishing it.

14. A. M. MacLeod, "Equality of Opportunity: Some Ambiguities in the Ideal." In Gary Dorsey, ed., *Equality and Freedom: International and Comparative Jurisprudence*, vol. 3 (Dobbs Ferry, N.Y.: 1977).

15. J. L. Lucas has gone so far as to argue that the concept of "equality" is so muddy and treacherous that it should be eliminated from political discourse altogether. See *The Principles of Politics* (Oxford: Clarendon Press, 1966), pp. 243–50; reprinted in Richard E. Flathman, ed., *Concepts in Social and Political Philosophy* (New York: Macmillan, 1973).

16. It is called "Victorian" but goes back a long way. The following advice is from a sermon by Bernardino of Siena in the early fifteenth century: "You should not give alms to every beggar and drunken vagabond; whence it is written (Ecclesiastes 12:5–6): 'Give to a righteous man and not to a sinner,' that is to the encouragement of sin; for many beggars haunt taverns and other disreputable places, setting examples of depravity." Brian S. Pullan, *A History of Early Renaissance Italy* (London: Allen Lane, 1973), p. 335.

4. Freedom

1. Isaiah Berlin, *Four Essays on Liberty* (New York: Oxford University Press, 1969), p. xxiii.

2. See, for example, Peter Winch, *The Idea of a Social Science, and Its Relation to Philosophy* (New York: Humanities Press, 1958).

3. For a good defense of this view, see Alexander Rosenberg, *Microeconomic Laws: A Philosophical Analysis* (Pittsburgh, Pa.: University of Pittsburgh Press, 1976).

4. A much better defense, by a belles-lettrist, is provided by Joseph Wood Krutch in his beautiful essay, "The Colloid and the Crystal," *The Best Nature Writings of Joseph Wood Krutch* (New York: Pocket Books, 1971).

5. A. H. Compton, *The Freedom of Man* (New Haven, Conn.: Yale University Press, 1935), and *The Human Meaning of Science* (Chapel Hill: University of North Carolina Press, 1940). It has been suggested that Niels Bohr's initial work on quantum mechanics was motivated by an ideological commitment to indeterminism; see Rosenberg, *Microeconomic Laws*, p. 207.

6. Popper's basic argument is in his *The Logic of Scientific Discovery* (London-New York: Harper & Row, 1968), first published in German in 1934. He gave a simple restatement in his Arthur Holly Compton Memorial Lecture, "Of Clouds and Clocks," at Washington University in 1965, re-

226   4. Freedom

printed in his *Objective Knowledge: An Evolutionary Approach* (Oxford: Clarendon Press, 1972).

7. K. R. Popper, *The Open Society and Its Enemies* (London: Routledge & Kegan Paul, 1945); *The Poverty of Historicism* (London: Routledge & Kegan Paul, 1957).

8. F. H. Knight, *Risk, Uncertainty, and Profit* (Boston and New York: Houghton Mifflin, 1921). Knight's most important writings on this issue are collected in *The Ethics of Competition and Other Essays* (New York: Kelley, 1935), and *Freedom and Reform: Essays in Economic and Social Philosophy* (New York: Harper, 1947). For a study of this aspect of Knight's thought, see Scott Gordon, "Frank Knight and the Tradition of Liberalism," *Journal of Political Economy* (1974).

9. Franz Neumann, "The Concept of Political Freedom," in Richard E. Flathman, ed., *Concepts in Social and Political Philosophy* (New York: Macmillan, 1973). This is a selection from Neumann's *The Democratic and the Authoritarian State* (New York: Free Press, 1957).

10. "Hegel's pronouncement that 'positive freedom' is achieved by an 'utter obedience or complete abnegation of one's own opinion and reasonings [meant] obedience to the Prussian state.' 'Only in being what the state wills us to be,' added his English disciple Bosanquet, 'can we speak, without contradiction, of being forced to be free.' " Herbert J. Muller, *Issues of Freedom: Paradoxes and Promises* (New York: Harper & Row, 1960), p. 16.

11. Neumann, "Concept of Political Freedom."

12. T. H. Green, *Works*, R. L. Nettleship, ed. (London: Longmans Green, 1893), 2:3.

13. Ruth Benedict, *The Chrysanthemum and the Sword* (New York: Meridian Books, 1967).

14. Berlin, *Four Essays.*

15. Gerald C. MacCallum, Jr., "Negative and Positive Freedom," *Philosophical Review* (1967).

16. F. A. Hayek, *The Road to Serfdom* (London: Routledge, 1944); *The Constitution of Liberty* (Chicago: University of Chicago Press, 1960).

17. Martin Bronfenbrenner, "Two Concepts of Economic Freedom," *Ethics* (April, 1955), p. 157.

18. A version of this that one encounters in the literature is that the nature of freedom is such that no sacrifice of it which is beneficial "really" reduces its own magnitude. Concerning this, Richard Flathman's comment is incisive: "Much thinking about positive freedom . . . encourages us to say not only that an interference or restriction is in the public interest, contributes to equality, welfare, morality, security, or whatever, but that it enhances freedom. If we submit to the temptation to talk this way, the felt

necessity of justifying the interference will have lost all basis. If our concepts really do encourage us to talk this way, we ought to change our concepts." Richard E. Flathman, ed., *Concepts in Social and Political Philosophy* (New York: Macmillan, 1973), p. 264.

5. Complementarity and Conflict Among Social Goods

1. A. H. Maslow, "The Theory of Human Motivation," *Psychological Review* (1943).

2. John Rawls, *A Theory of Justice* (Cambridge, Mass.: Harvard University Press, 1971).

3. See Arthur M. Okun, *Equality and Efficiency: The Big Tradeoff* (Washington, D.C.: Brookings, 1975); and "Further Thoughts on Equality and Efficiency," in Colin D. Campbell, ed., *Income Redistribution* (Washington, D.C.: American Enterprise Institute, 1977).

4. Scott Gordon, "Social Science and Value Judgments," *Canadian Journal of Economics* (1977).

6. The Distribution and Control of Coercive Power

1. In a representative democracy it requires only one vote more than 50 percent to elect a representative (less when there is more than one candidate) and only one more than 50 percent of the representatives to pass a law. It is, therefore, possible for a law to have the approval of only 25 percent of the electorate, or less if a plurality of votes is sufficient to elect a representative in more than two-party contests.

2. W. L. Burn, *The Age of Equipose: A Study of the Mid-Victorian Generation* (London: Allen & Unwin, 1964), p. 238n. Burn points out generally that a great deal of the personal coercion of this period was "social" rather than legal, and that much state action was undertaken with the aim of increasing personal freedom.

3. J. H. Randall, *The Making of the Modern Mind* (Boston and New York: Houghton Mifflin, 1940), p. 283.

4. H. C. Simons, *Economic Policy for a Free Society* (Chicago: University of Chicago Press, 1948), pp. 33ff. Simons strongly argued that associations restrict the intellectual freedom of their members not only by making specific rules, but, more commonly and more insidiously, by insisting on "loyalty," that is, uncritical support of the association's aims and practices. In the USSR it is a definite crime to "slander the Soviet State," but effective

coercion need not be so specific; social ostracism or disapproval, reduction of chances to advance in the hierarchy of the organization, and other things work powerfully also. All associations tend to make intellectual eunuchs of their members when undiscriminating loyalty to the church, the firm, the family, or whatever, is insisted upon. Most universities remain havens of intellectual freedom because the vital interests of the organization, as an organization, are not immediately affected by the views of its scholars, though this freedom is far from complete and is always exposed to erosion because of the university's dependence on financing from gifts and grants.

5. For a summary of the main provisions of the act, see *European Industrial Relations Review* (May 1976).

6. *Wall Street Journal*, March 10, 1977.

7. *New York Times*, February 2, 1977.

8. *Indianapolis Star*, March 19, 1977.

9. Charles K. Rowley and Alan T. Peacock, *Welfare Economics: A Liberal Restatement* (New York: Wiley, 1975). This book is a sustained attack on Paretian economics for its neglect of the value of freedom.

10. One of the reasons why the university remains a locus of great freedom is that its hierarchical organization is exceptionally loose. Assistant professors do not take orders from associates or associates from full professors. None of the three are under much supervision by departmental chairmen, deans, or presidents so, at the levels where scholarly activity is carried on, the system is as close to anarchy as is compatible with the elementary requirements of order.

11. In this discussion, it is obvious that I have Britain mainly in mind. In North America the scenario was different because, except for the plantation economy of the South and the seignorial system of French Canada, land was too widely dispersed to permit the formation of an aristocracy along European lines.

12. Eugene Rotwein, ed., *David Hume: Writings on Economics* (Madison, Wis.: University of Wisconsin Press, 1970), pp. ci–cii.

13. Milton Friedman, *Capitalism and Freedom* (Chicago: University of Chicago Press, 1962).

14. The only rational preference ordering for dictatorship is as follows: First preference: the dictator is to be *me*. Second preference: if not me, someone *like me*. Third preference: if not me or someone like me, someone who is *ineffectual*.

15. The classic statement is Mark Twain's first book, coauthored with C. D. Warner, *The Gilded Age* (1873). William Dean Howells was making no simple simile when he described Twain as "the Lincoln of our literature."

16. Those who believe that there is a homogeneous "Chicago School" of

political philosophy should compare the views, on this point, of two of its supposed priests: Henry C. Simons and Milton Friedman.

17. I use the conditional expression because statistical calculations of the distribution of property neglect human capital, its most rapidly growing and most power-conferring form.

18. The classic delineation of this development is A. A. Berle, Jr., and G. C. Means, *The Modern Corporation and Private Property* (New York: Macmillan, 1932). Some other well-known works are James Burnham, *The Managerial Revolution* (London: Penguin, 1941), and J. K. Galbraith, *The New Industrial State* (Boston: Houghton Mifflin, 1967). In the limit, there may be no real shareholders at all. If a corporation buys up all of its outstanding voting stock from its own funds, as some insurance companies and other financial institutions have done, it is then the legal owner of itself, a bizarre extension of the legal construction of the corporate entity as a person, and one that makes managerial control complete.

19. This, and its implications, were pointed out two decades ago by Paul P. Harbrecht, SJ, in *Pension Funds and Economic Power* (New York: Twentieth Century Fund, 1959). Since then the funds have grown enormously.

20. The classic statement of this, the "iron law of oligarchy," is Robert Michels, *Political Parties: A Sociological Study of the Oligarchic Tendencies of Modern Democracy* (New York: Collier, 1962; first published in German, 1911.)

21. Franz Neumann, "The Concept of Political Freedom," in Richard E. Flathman, ed., *Concepts in Social and Political Philosophy* (New York: Macmillan, 1973).

22. W. J. Bouwsma, *Venice and the Defense of Republican Liberty* (Berkeley, Calif.: University of California Press, 1968), pp. 149–50.

23. Marcus Cunliffe, *The Nation Takes Shape: 1789–1837* (Chicago: University of Chicago Press, 1959), p. 34.

24. Friedman, *Capitalism and Freedom.*

Index